Famous Speakers & Writers

During the past 100 years, these people have been among the world's most effective motivational speakers and writers. The names marked with checks are active in speaking to the financial products and services industries today.

Steve Allen✓
Alan W. Altmann✓
Claude Bristol
Les Brown✓
Jack Canfield✓
Dale Carnegie
Deepak Chopra
Winston Churchill
George S. Clason
Jan Cooper✓
Stephen R. Covey✓
Robert Dames✓
Wayne Dyer✓
Sidney Friedman✓
Mahatma Gandi
Rev. Billy Graham
' Roy M. Henry✓
Napoleon Hill
Coach Lou Holtz✓
Tom Hopkins✓
L. Ron Hubbard
Rev. Ike
Michael S. Kindberg✓
Martin Luther King
Art Linkletter
Nelson Mandella
Og Mandino
Harvey McKay✓
Arthur H. "Red" Motley
Jawahrial Nehru
Earl Nightingale
Rev. Norman Vincent Peale
Ronald Reagan
Anthony Robbins✓
Eleanor Roosevelt
Franklin D. Roosevelt
Rev. Robert Schuller
Fulton J. Sheen
Blair Singer✓
W. Clement Stone
Brian Tracy✓
Dennis Waitley✓
Maharishi Mahesh Yogi
Zig Ziglar✓

story of the Amway company's success, and the book was a national best-seller. *Success: How Every Man and Woman Can Achieve It* by Michael Korda describes "techniques, tricks, styles and shortcuts." Korda is also the author of *Power: How to Get It, How to Use It. Success: You Can Make It Happen* by Dr. Lila Swell, is based on her educational course for helping young adults obtain richer and more fulfilling lives.

Editor's Top Picks. I recommend the following 10 volumes, after the main works of W. Clement Stone, Napoleon Hill, Dale Carnegie and Norman Vincent Peale.

• Sidney Friedman, *The Wonderful Wizard In You*
• Maxwell Maltz, *Psycho Cybernetics*
• Wayne Dyer, *Your Erroneous Zones*
• Tom Hopkins, *How to Master the Art of Selling*
• Stephen Brennen, *Successfully Yours*
• Bjorn Secher, *Appointment with Success*
• Margery Wilson, *Kinetic Psycho-Dynamics*
• David Schwartz, *The Magic of Thinking Big*
• Claude Bristol, *The Magic of Believing*
• G. Worthington Hipple, *Sell Yourself Rich*

Conclusion

A general overview of all four types of success motivation books leads to the following conclusions, which are not absolute:

• *Self-help books tend to be of greater value if they are published by established publishers.* Beware of self-aid books which are printed independently or by companies seeking to promote their products of services.

• *Personal motivation books can be of interest and use.* Most are well-written and based upon proven techniques and practices.

• *Inspirational guidance books are often promotion vehicles for vari-*

ous *"religious" publishers and authors.* Others are possibly more genuine. Some are of value in conveying hope and helping to establish faith in oneself.

• *Sales improvement books are valuable training tools for anyone involved in sales.* These generally can help the reader increase his or her sales totals by becoming better organized.

Many financial planners have favorite success motivation books. My favorite is the success classic *Success Through a Positive Mental Attitude* by Napoleon Hill and W. Clement Stone. Second is *Sell Yourself Rich* by G. Worthington Hipple. Hipple keeps repeating this theme: "Unusual action creates unusual results."[19]

It has been my observation that most success motivation books contain padding. Their wisdom can often be distilled and recorded in much less space for an equally effective learning experience. For instance, the book *How to Advertise Yourself*, by Maxwell B. Sackheim uses 192 pages to expound on five basic steps. Other publishers might have required around 486 pages.

Success authors make their points well through the use of illustrations, examples and stories, plus case histories. A prospective success motivation book buyer and reader should be selective.

Everyone's a Motivator

Rev. Alan W. "Big Al" Altmann, a former Million Dollar Round Table member who became a minister, says, "Many 'has beens' from show business, politics and sports end up as motivational speakers. Some Olympic athletes, like Mary Lou Retton, go straight from Olympic participation to the motivational speaking circuits. The syndicated 'radio pitchman' Paul Harvey is often booked as a motivational speaker. Motivational speaking and writing is seen as a way to exploit a 'half-name' or 'fading name' and still generate income."

Rev. Altmann adds, "Many former celebrities 'turn religious'

Dr. Jan and Steve Forbes at a convention in Washington DC

Dr. Jan and General Williamson

Jan Cooper Thinks Peale Was An Example For All Of Us

Jan Cooper, artist, educator, writer, and TV personality, known as "The Renaissance Man," thinks, "Both Rev. Dr. Norman Vincent Peale and his wife, Ruth, have been an inspiration to me. They are examples for everyone."

Cooper adds, "I know Ruth Stafford Peale better than I knew her husband. But of course I knew him by his great work. He helped millions of people and many of them felt as if they knew him personally. As if he was their confidant and close friend. I hope one day I can do for others what they did for me."

JAN COOPER

In 1978, I found another art form to fall in love with. I combined my art with professional speaking.

Cavett Robert, the founder of the National Speakers Association said " Jan, you were born with Divine Dissatisfaction ".

Thank you Cavett, without your encouragement, I could not have come this far.

Special thanks to everyone in NSA.

Dr. Jan and Dr. Robert A. Schuller

CREATE, SELL, AND BECOME RICH

WEALTH AND WISDOM
AT YOUR FINGER TIPS

By

Dr. Jan Cooper

ISBN: 978-1-304-28558-4 (PB)
978-1-304-28559-1 (HB)

Dedication

I dedicate this book to those who use their time wisely to make their dreams come true.

WHAT TIME IS LEFT IN YOUR LIFE?

Let's just say on average that humans live around 96 years. Let's boil it down to one 24-hour day. We are born at midnight and we are going to die at midnight. Every hour equals 4 years. Exercise: Shade in everything that you have already used up!

AM

12:00 am	12:15 am	12:30 am	12:45 am	1:00 am	(4)
1:00 am	1:15 am	1:30 am	1:45 am	2:00 am	(8)
2:00 am	2:15 am	2:30 am	2:45 am	3:00 am	(12)
3:00 am	3:15 am	3:30 am	3:45 am	4:00 am	(16)
4:00 am	4:15 am	4:30 am	4:45 am	5:00 am	(20)
5:00 am	5:15 am	5:30 am	5:45 am	6:00 am	(24)
6:00 am	6:15 am	6:30 am	6:45 am	7:00 am	(28)
7:00 am	7:15 am	7:30 am	7:45 am	8:00 am	(32)
8:00 am	8:15 am	8:30 am	8:45 am	9:00 am	(36)
9:00 am	9:15 am	9:30 am	9:45 am	10:00 am	(40)
10:00 am	10:15 am	10:30 am	10:45 am	11:00 am	(44)
11:00 am	11:15 am	11:30 am	11:45 am	12:00 pm	(48)

PM

12:00 pm	12:15 pm	12:30 pm	12:45 pm	1:00 pm	(52)
1:00 pm	1:15 pm	1:30 pm	1:45 pm	2:00 pm	(56)

2:00 pm	2:15 am	2:30 am	2:45 am	3:00 am	(60)
3:00 pm	3:15 pm	3:30 pm	3:45 pm	4:00 pm	(64)
4:00 pm	4:15 pm	4:30 pm	4:45 pm	5:00 pm	(68)
5:00 pm	5:15 pm	5:30 pm	5:45 pm	6:00 pm	(72)
6:00 pm	6:15 pm	6:30 pm	6:45 pm	7:00 pm	(76)
7:00 pm	7:15 pm	7:30 pm	7:45 pm	8:00 pm	(80)
8:00 pm	8:15 pm	8:30 pm	8:45 pm	9:00 pm	(84)
9:00 pm	9:15 pm	9:30 pm	9:45 pm	10:00 pm	(88)
10:00 pm	10:15 pm	10:30 pm	10:45 pm	11:00 pm	(92)
11:00 pm	11:15 pm	11:30 pm	11:45 pm	12:00 pm	(96)

GIVE YOURSELF THE GIFT OF LIFE!

Now you know you may have only a few years left to do what you were meant to do. Turn your life into a Masterpiece and live your dream.

Introduction

Yes, you can Create, Sell, and become Rich. A Holistic approach to transforming your life: PHYSICALLY, MENTALLY, SPIRITUALLY, and FINANCIALLY!

Get in the habit of walking, running, skipping, hopping, riding a bicycle, playing golf, just doing something physical everyday. Keep your mind alert by reading, writing, studying, and learning something new everyday. Pray, meditate, read the Bible, read success stories, and continually search for WISDOM!

When you do the above you will achieve PEAK PERFORMANCE, feel more relaxed, and improve your productivity! You will become more AWARE of who you are and what you want. You will set goals and put your plans into ACTION! You will start thinking about who you want for a coach, mentor, or consultant. You will achieve your DREAMS! You will CREATE, SELL, and become RICH!

You are your own artist. You are your own brushes. You are your own colors. You are the STAR of your life. Turn your life into a MASTERPIECE! WISDOM and WEALTH are at your FINGER-TIPS. Dr. Norman Vincent Peale once said, "Anything of worth requires discipline."

I want you to know, every babystep you take , you are in my prayers!

Dr. Jan

What Is On the $1.00 Bill?

*M*any, many, many years ago I read these words about the dollar bill. I have no idea who wrote them. But, they inspired and impressed me, as I hope they do you.

Take out a one-dollar bill and look at it. (Go ahead, for real, get one out.)

The one-dollar bill you're looking at first came off the presses in 1957 in its present design. This so-called paper money is, in fact, a cotton linen, with red and blue minute silk fibers running through it. It is actually material. We've all washed it without it falling apart. A special blend of ink is used, the contents of which we will never know. It is printed over with symbols, starched to make it water resistant and pressed to give it that nice, crisp look.

If you look at the front of the bill, you will see:

$ The United States Treasury Seal; on the top, you will see the scales for balance—a balanced budget.
$ In the center, you have a carpenter's T square, a tool used for an even cut.
$ Underneath is the key to the United States Department of the Treasury.

That's all pretty easy to figure out, but what is on the back of that dollar bill is something we should all know. If you turn the bill over, you will see:

$ Two circles; both circles, together, comprise the Great Seal of the United States. The First Continental Congress requested that Benjamin Franklin and a group of men come up with a seal. It took them four years to accomplish this task and another two years to get it approved.

$ If you look at the left-hand circle, you will see a pyramid. Notice that the face is lighted and the western side is dark. This country was just beginning. We had not begun to explore the West or decided what we could do for Western civilization.

$ At the base of the pyramid is the Roman numeral for 1776.

$ If you look at the right-hand circle and check it carefully, you will learn that it is on every national cemetery in the United States. It is also on the Parade of Flags Walkway at the Florida National Cemetery in Bushnell, Florida, and is the centerpiece of most heroes' monuments. Slightly modified, it is the seal of the President of the United States and it is always visible whenever he speaks. Yet no one knows what the symbols mean.

$ The bald eagle was selected as a symbol for victory for two reasons:

> **First**, he is not afraid of a storm; he is strong and smart enough to soar above it.
>
> **Second**, he wears no material crown. We had just broken from the king of England.

$ The pyramid is uncapped, again signaling that we were not even close to being finished. Inside the capstone, you have the all-seeing eye, an ancient symbol for divinity. It was Franklin's belief that one man couldn't do it alone, but a group of men, with the help of God, could do anything.

$ "IN GOD WE TRUST" is on this currency.

$ In Latin, above the pyramid, ANNUIT COEPTIS, means "God has favored our undertaking."

$ The Latin below the pyramid, NOVUS ORDO SECLORUM, means "a new order has begun."

$ Also, notice that the shield is unsupported. This country can now stand on its own.

$ *At the top of that shield, you have a white bar, signaling Congress, a unifying factor. We were coming together as one nation.*

$ *In the eagle's beak, you will read, "E PLURIBUS UNUM," meaning "one nation from many people."*

$ *Above the eagle, you have thirteen stars, representing the thirteen original colonies and any clouds of misunderstanding rolling away. Again, we were coming together as one.*

$ *Notice what the eagle holds in his talons. He holds an olive branch and arrows. This country wants peace, but we will never be afraid to fight to preserve peace.*

$ *The eagle always wants to face the olive branch, but in times of war, his gaze turns toward the arrows.*

$ *They say that the number 13 is an unlucky number. This is almost a worldwide belief. You will usually never see a room numbered 13, or any hotels or motels with a thirteenth floor. But think about this:*

    ♥ *Thirteen original colonies*
    ♥ *Thirteen signers of the Declaration of Independence*
    ♥ *Thirteen stripes on our flag*
    ♥ *Thirteen steps on the pyramid*
    ♥ *Thirteen letters in Latin above the pyramid*
    ♥ *Thirteen letters in "E Pluribus Unum,"*
    ♥ *Thirteen stars above the eagle*
    ♥ *Thirteen plumes of feathers on each span of the eagle's wings*
    ♥ *Thirteen bars on that shield*
    ♥ *Thirteen leaves on the olive branch*
    ♥ *Thirteen fruits, and, if you look closely,*
    ♥ *Thirteen arrows*

$ *And for minorities:*
    ♥ *The Thirteenth Amendment*

Too many people don't know this. Too many veterans have given up too much to ever let the meaning fade. Many veterans remember coming home to an America that didn't care. Too many veterans never came home at all. If you don't tell anyone what is on the back of the one-dollar bill and what it stands for, who will?

TABLE OF CONTENTS

Daniel 2:21
And he changeth. "the times and the seasons: he removeth kings
and setteth up kings: he giveth wisdom unto the wise, and knowledge
to them that know understanding."

Part One
Your Left Wing—Creativity

C reativity drives success. But there's more to it than that. Before you turn the next page, I want you to promise not to panic when you see the long version of my Success Equation. Sure, it looks formidable at first glance, but in reality, it's not only easy to understand, it's well worth the small effort required because it's a tool of life-changing value.

So stick with me, and I'll explain how you can apply this powerhouse equation to remold your life and make your dreams come true.

The intervening chapters will give you insights that will make the equation easier to apply to your own life and everyday decisions.

Here's the long version of the Success Equation:

$$\text{TCFWY} = \text{HW} + \text{T} + \text{N} + \text{M} + \text{AQ} + \text{S} + \text{H} + 7\text{S} \times \text{PPP}^2 \times \text{P}^{10}$$

1 Corinthians 15:33
"Be not deceived: evil communications
corrupt good manners."

CHAPTER 1

People Who Have Influenced My Life

D r. Norman Vincent Peale and his wife, Ruth, W. Clement Stone, and Robert H. Schuller have greatly influenced my life. When I was a young boy, my hero was Superman. As an adult, my heroes have been Dr. Norman Vincent Peale and his wife, Ruth, W. Clement Stone, and Robert H. Schuller. In the next few pages, I am going to share some of their teachings that I believe will add to my Success Equation and help people live a fulfilling life. Read their words carefully; I've selected them with care in hopes that they will have a lasting effect on your life, as they have on mine.

Robert H. Schuller shares these guiding words:

Finding and following God's plan for your life is the soundest, surest way to self-confidence. Already, God is revealing to you His plan for your life. He has started working in your life. Be sure, God finishes what He started! Being confident of this very thing, that he which hath begun "a good work in you will perform it until the day of Jesus Christ." (Philippians 1:6). God often allows problems to shake us up in order to get us out of a rut and onto the beautiful road He has planned for us.

Paint a mental picture of the new you! You are going to change. You are changing now. You will become the person you've always wanted to be; believe this. Now discard old mental pictures of yourself. These old portraits are past history. Replace them with the dream portrait of the person you want to become.

Disadvantaged, defected, and discouraged people are learning how to change their lives, their futures, and their destinies. Now it's your turn to stop failing and start succeeding. Discover the better idea God has for your life. You are God's idea, and God only dreams up beautiful ideas. He's expecting great things from you. Cooperate! Believe in yourself now and draw the possibilities out of your being.

I believe these words of inspiration can help anyone, no matter how advanced they are. Yes, God has a plan for you. Only you know in your heart the plan that God is preparing you for. Now prepare for your transformation.

W. Clement Stone, one of the world's wealthiest men, had this to say:

You, too, can succeed by learning and applying two principles that were never taught in any school and which guarantee the achievement of any goal that doesn't violate the laws of God or the rights of one's fellow man. *Recognize*, *relate*, *assimilate*, and *apply* principles from what you see, hear, read, think, or experience. Use your conscious mind to tap the vast powers of your subconscious. Study, think, plan, and act.

Motivation is that which induces action or determines choice. It is that which provides a motive. A motive is an urge within the individual, such as an instinct, emotion, habit, impulse, or idea that incites him to action. It is the hope or other force that moves the individual to attempt to produce specific results. Be ready to recognize and grasp each opportunity when it comes.

Whenever you don't feel like doing something, repeat to yourself, "Do it now!" and act immediately. A positive mental attitude is necessary for achieving worthwhile success. Apply the golden rule, and aim high.

Remember, anything in life worth having is worth working for; anything worth working for is worth praying for. Prayer is man's greatest power. Those who pray daily for desirable achievements intensify their desires. With every adversity, there is a seed of an equivalent or greater benefit for those who have a positive mental attitude.

It is imperative that you develop the habit of examining your reactions to individuals, circumstances, and events, and to the reactions of individuals and groups to what you say, write, or do. To acquire the true riches of life, it is essential that you develop a pleasing personality; pleasing to yourself and to others. When you have a problem with another person, analyze the situation to help bring about the desired result.

Now I can see why he was one of the world's wealthiest men.

Mr. and Mrs. "Positive Thinking"

Dr. Norman Vincent Peale shared some of his greatest teachings: In the very necessary business of solving personal problems, it is important, first of all, to realize that the power to solve them correctly is inherent within you. Second, it is necessary to work out and actualize a plan. Spiritual and emotional helplessness is a definite reason for the failure of many people to meet their personal problems successfully.

Faith supplies lasting power. It contains dynamics to keep one going when the going is hard. Anybody can keep going when the going is good, but some extra ingredient is needed to enable you to keep fighting when it seems that everything is against you.

In attempting emotional control, the daily practice of healing techniques is of paramount importance. Emotional control cannot be gained in any magical way. You cannot develop it by merely reading a book, although that is often helpful. The only sure method is by working at it regularly, scientifically, and by developing creative faith.

Change your mental habits to those of belief instead of disbelief. Learn to expect, not to doubt. In so doing, you bring everything into the realm of possibility. This does not mean that by believing, you are necessarily going to get everything you want. Perhaps that would not be good for you. When you put your trust in God, he guides your mind so you do not want things that are bad for you or that is inharmonious with God's will.

Ruth Stafford Peale

Dr. Peale's wife had this to say: "There is a power within each of us that intervenes in human affairs, sometimes providing answers to problems, sometimes exerting a subtle influence on thought processes, sometimes arranging or rearranging the complex pattern of human existence so that desirable goals can be reached. I believe there is such a force, and I believe it is a blessing from God."

Jan and his wife Sandy

CHAPTER 2
Discover Your Inner Gold Mine

C ould it be that you want your life to be fun? Customized? Perhaps you want it to be an easily followed trail. Create your own map. Then pave your way to heaven on earth. Psyche yourself up about your future. Don't mess around wasting your talents and abilities. Your ideas are fragile. If you don't write them down and put them into action, they will just waste away into broken wishes. Nothing written down, nothing accomplished.

Make the hidden obvious. Maximize your knowledge to bring out your fullest potential. Tell your story by making your dream work for you. Knowledge, courage, and direction are just a few steps away; add them to your power. Get the most out of your life. Remember all those things you dreamed of and always said you would do. Prove it to yourself, and have a love affair with life.

Take Time to Discover the Power Inside Your Skin

So, what's new? You are changing. In fact, change and learning to live with change is everything. Yes, you are in control of your destiny. A new concept is born to shorten your path with better answers, so you can keep your sanity.

Yes, you know all of the answers. But a simple tool was created to shorten your path. It is an equation that all can follow.

Prepare for the millennium. It will add sizzle to your life, if followed. Don't be just a face in the crowd. Your words, your actions, and your decisions give you power.

7

By being honest with yourself and using a simple tool—a simple mathematical equation—your blindness will be opened to vision. So get off your bum and create a new you for the MILLENNIUM. It's never too late. This is your year. So stick to your resolutions and create and grow rich—physically, mentally, spiritually, and financially. Adopt a holistic viewpoint to help heal your life.

Release the Inner Child

Babies look at the world with eyes filled with wonder and they live in the moment. If they're hungry, they want food *now*; if they're tired, they sleep now, or make the whole world aware of their displeasure at being kept awake by inconsiderate big people.

Babies put everything in their mouths because that's the keenest way they can experience something new. As they grow older, bad experiences make them more careful of what goes in their mouths, and their ability to live only in the present moment begins to fade.

As adults, we can't regain a baby's ability to absorb new knowledge at incredible speed, without returning to the baby's automatic reflex of popping everything in our mouths. But to achieve our highest level of creativity, we must release the inner child. When we do that, we're able to live in the present. We're able to look at everything and everyone with eyes that are always fresh, full of wonder, and eager to grasp new insights.

How do we release the inner child? Though the concept is simple, the realization of it takes a little time and a lot of effort. Concentrate on the present moment by pushing aside all distractions. To enable this, set up a system that will remind you of other obligations and opportunities so you don't have to think about them in the present moment. This allows you to throw yourself totally into making the most of the present moment.

Happiness Is Internal

As long as you depend on someone else for your happiness, your state of mind is precarious. Worse yet, if your happiness depends on stuff, on mere things that you can (or wish you could) buy, lasting happiness will elude you. Of course, some material gains will momentarily make you happy, but you'll quickly find that anticipation exceeds realization.

Build your happiness within yourself, independent of any other person or what you possess, or don't have. Does this mean you will love your special person less? On the contrary, building internal happiness means you can love him or her more. When your relationship is freed of desperate, emotional dependence, you will be enormously more able to love your special person for who he or she really is. A wonderful new world of happy communication can flow between you as a result of your newfound internal happiness and emotional security.

Discover Your Talent, Discover Your Potential, Discover the Gold Mine Within

Keep your mind busy. It seems that my mind is always in a state of motion even when I'm asleep.

Asking questions is what will give you the results and answers you want. Often, while asleep, dozing, napping, opening a book, running into a stranger, or working on a new project, you will receive the answers you need for your new invention, book, poem, song, painting, or other creative projects.

Celebrate Your Uniqueness

Prize your uniqueness; dwell on it; develop it; flaunt it. There are upwards of six billion human beings on this planet—but only one you. Although all of us share many things with every other human being, we are incredibly complex organisms who have been subjected to an enormous quantity of different experiences. As a result, each of us views the world from a different perspective. Your vision is not my vision. We have great powers of communication, yet we cannot communicate all of our uniqueness.

In our teen years, most of us want to be just like everybody else. We tend to hide anything that would make us look or seem different. The most accurate measure of maturity is how willing we are to recognize, dwell on, and display our uniqueness in socially acceptable ways.

Open Your Mind Wider

We have to shut out distractions so that we can focus on our main goals. But this need must be balanced against another vital need—to keep our minds as open as possible so that we can see new opportunities and avoid new dangers.

How do you open your mind wider? There are so many ways. I've split them into two categories: conventional, or off-line, and online, digitally via computer.

Off-Line

1. **Spend a little time at least once a month at a good newsstand, or in the periodical section of your library.**

    The number of magazines being published today is astonishing; all of them are tightly focused on a single area of interest. Look them over. You'll probably find some that will point you toward new directions of growth.

2. **Turn your automobile into a learning center at no cost.**

    Many public libraries have cassette albums, complete readings of nonfiction subjects as well as of novels and plays. Devote your morning commute to self-improvement; it's when your mind is freshest and most receptive to learning. Too many of us waste our morning commute fuming at dumb drivers or poking along in a daze. Use this precious alone time to learn a new language or other skill, explore the plays of Shakespeare, march out of Asia with Xenophon, renew your acquaintance with Mark Twain and Hemingway, learn about other cultures, other countries, other times. In a lighter vein, you could also hear Sherlock Holmes and Spenser defeat the bad guys, or enjoy some other genre novels: romance, adventure, thriller, western, mystery, or sci-fi, or a mainstream best seller. By turning your boring commute into an exciting learning experience, you'll arrive at work mentally refreshed and eager to begin the day's work. The difference will soon show up in your paycheck.

3. **Use your evening commute to listen to talk shows.**
   Most of it is drivel, so use your push buttons to switch from one show to another. If they're all the usual brainless chatter, go for some relaxing music or finish that exciting novel.

4. **Scan the new book section of your public library.**
   A thousand new nonfiction books are published in the United States every week, and that includes only books put out by trade publishers. In addition, even more are published privately or on the Internet.

5. **Listen to different kinds of music.**

6. **Read different poets.**

7. **Become an expert on a new subject unrelated to your work.**

8. **Read history and philosophy. Read the great books.**

Online

1. **Surf the 'Net.**
   The Internet offers access to millions of Web sites devoted to every imaginable kind of knowledge. Learning to use the 'Net's search engines to find anything you want to know is fun and easy.

2. **Amazon.com (http://www.amazon.com) lists more than a million different titles for sale.**

   They not only make it easy to search for exactly what you want, they tell you more than any other Web site does about any book you might be considering. Two other major online bookstores are:
   http://www.barnesandnoble.com/
   http://www.borders.com

3. **Look into buying what you need on the 'Net.**

   It's the best place to find good deals on insurance and just about everything else.

4. **Also check out selling what you no longer need.**

   Whether it be cars, cameras, or camping gear, Amazon.com and eBay.com are the two largest Web sites conducting millions of auctions every day of everything imaginable.

5. **Get involved in chat rooms.**

   You can make new friends and intensify your sense of uniqueness by expressing yourself on any subject that comes to mind.

The Success Equation, short version:
$$PF \times MD \times SP + FS = \text{Joyful Living}$$

Physical Factors times Mental Discipline times Spiritual Power plus Financial Success equals **Joyful Living**.

CHAPTER 3
Physical Factors

T alk to your doctor before you begin any exercise program, especially if you're over thirty and not in great shape.

The Goal Is Glowing Health, Not Merely the Avoidance of Disease

Years ago, I talked to a lady who claimed that the only factor in health is what you eat. She insisted that disease, accidents, genetic conditions, the air you breathe, and the amount and kind of exercise you get—or don't get—all have nothing to do with your health. In her view, the only thing that counts is what you eat. Not surprisingly, this lady was somewhat overweight and not in what appeared to be glowing health. In spite of what she wanted to believe, we are not as simple as she supposed. Our lives are multidimensional. We are incredibly complicated.

Consider scurvy, a serious disease caused by a deficiency of vitamin C. Scurvy is rare today—and almost impossible to get in most of the civilized world—because it's easily corrected simply by eating fresh fruits or vegetables. However, for centuries, it was a plague on the sea. Sailors on long voyages often died of it. Without knowing why, the English navy discovered that having their sailors drink some lime juice every day prevented scurvy. Although vitamin C deficiencies show up more dramatically than most do, glowing health requires the regular supply of a long list of natural substances.

Of course, many factors besides diet contribute to glowing health. For a few years, people who smoke can seem to be in the best of health because they're young; the same with people who abuse alcohol or other drugs.

Glowing health comes from taking care of an incredibly complex organism—your body. Although we still have much to learn about the treatment of disease, medical research reveals new knowledge about the human body every day. Even more hopeful, research and medical training is slowly swinging toward prevention rather than cure.

Although we don't know everything about how to achieve glowing health, many things are already clear. We know that being overweight and smoking shortens life by increasing the chances of cancer and cardiovascular disease (heart attacks and other diseases of the blood circulation system).

We know that being a couch potato shortens life. We know that without movement and exercise, the body decays. Recently published studies show that it's never too late to increase the amount of exercise in your life. Suitable exercise programs for ninety-year-old people who were confined to wheelchairs have, in many cases, enabled them to walk again.

Another study shows that short-term memory and thinking ability improve as the direct result of physical exercise. Although this particular study was conducted on sedentary people over age sixty-five, the same result would probably be obtained by getting couch potatoes of any age to exercise regularly.

The mind/body connection is highly complex; signals flow both ways via many channels. What we eat, drink, breathe, and especially what we think and the emotions we feel, pour chemical messengers into the bloodstream.

These messenger hormones can affect us powerfully. If you're a passenger in a car or an airplane and something happens to make you think your life is in danger, what happens to you internally? You're still sitting there unharmed, but hormones are alerting every cell in your body to get ready to fight or flee for your life. But there's no one to fight and no place to flee, so all you can do is feel fear. Usually, you escape whatever scared you without injury, causing other hormone messengers to call off the alert, and your fear subsides.

What does this prove? That your mind, interpreting what your eyes see and your ears hear, can powerfully influence your body.

Most human beings engage in constant self-talk throughout their waking moments. All this self-talk is divided into two vastly different kinds: it's either negative or positive.

Your self-talk influences your body just as powerfully as do the fight or flee hormones; self-talk just works more slowly and less dramatically. But over time, your self-talk determines everything from your health, your success in every aspect of your life, and even the length of your life.

So if you want to live a long, vigorous life in glowing health, free of disease, dwell on positive things about yourself, your abilities, and your future. Eat wisely, exercise regularly, avoid tobacco and other dangerous drugs, and strictly limit your alcohol intake. Positive self-talk will enable you to do all this almost effortlessly.

Health Comes at a Price

To achieve anything worthwhile, we must sacrifice some less important things. If your favorite thing—something you do every day and all day on the weekend—is to plop down in front of the TV and munch some tasty tidbits, this habit stands solidly between you and glowing health. Cut down on this mindless waste of your health and life. Use some of this time to exercise, either outside or, if you can't stand to miss some TV event, exercise on a rowing machine or bicycle in front of the tube. Look in local throwaway papers, or check the online auctions at Amazon.com or eBay.com and you'll be surprised at how cheap you can buy home exercise equipment.

Take Small Bites

If you have some lifestyle habits that are dangerous to your health, consider changing them slowly. It can be a real shock to the body to crank up a heavy exercise schedule, switch to a low-fat diet, and stop smoking all in the same month. Unless you have extraordinary discipline, trying to move that fast will come to a crashing halt as your system fights for equilibrium.

If you're out of shape and in need of a drastic overhaul, remember, it took years of neglect to do that to yourself. Give your body a break and work out a detailed plan for accomplishing all of your objectives. Be sure to set reasonable goals that you can achieve and feel like a winner, rather than tough goals you won't reach, leaving you feeling discouraged. The vital thing is to start.

If your diet needs overhauling to get rid of high fat, you may find it easier to switch one food at a time. In other words, as one person puts it, train down to low fat. If you're a couch potato right now and want to get in shape, start by walking for a mile every morning, and increase it as your body adjusts.

Set Your Goals Right

They're too high if you don't passionately believe you can achieve them. They're too low if they don't excite you. If you have a long way to go, take it in small steps.

Small Steps

Lay out a program of increasing difficulty so you're gradually increasing physical capacity, skill level, and knowledge that can keep up with the gradually increasing level of accomplishment you demand of yourself. In setting small steps, always aim for wins that push you a bit to achieve.

However, avoid setting your small steps so high that you often fail to reach them in spite of a strong effort. This tends to de-motivate you. Remember, the basic purpose of breaking your large goal down into small steps is to keep you motivated. Organize your small steps for success, not failure; set them up to keep you encouraged.

Review your progress at regular times—weekly at first, perhaps switching to monthly review after you have made substantial progress and are thoroughly committed. Regular review is essential—skipping reviews is a sign that your purpose is in trouble. If you are struggling, ask yourself if you really want to reach the goal in question. If you still do, build more rewards into your small-step program, and consider intensifying your efforts to increase your motivation in other ways. For example, can you enter any competitions to help you reach your goal?

Also consider making yourself accountable to someone for your progress.

As your achievement drive continues, you will learn which area of development needs more attention—and perhaps more time.

Pumping Iron

Some commercial gyms are open 24/7/365. In other words, they never close. If 3 a.m. is the most convenient time for you to start working out, go for it. Lifting weights is the premier way to build strength, but it doesn't build endurance unless accompanied by aerobic exercise such as running on the treadmill. A powerfully-built bodybuilder failed the physical at the Los Angeles Police Academy a few years ago. He was amazed. In his concentration on lifting heavier and heavier weights to bulk up his muscles, he had entirely neglected aerobic training. The man could bench press 500 pounds, but he couldn't run 500 feet without stopping to catch his breath.

That flunked him. His was an unusual case; most bodybuilders balance weight training with aerobic exercise.

Weight training is the easiest exercise to take in graduated steps. You not only can choose whatever weight you want, you have the choice of how many repetitions you perform. On some exercises, you'll do two or three sets of six or ten repetitions each. On another exercise machine, you may do one set of forty-five repetitions. You can increase the weight or repetitions as your strength grows. Once you're accustomed to weight training—which takes a newcomer perhaps two weeks, going every other day—your body will tell you when to increase the challenge of an exercise. That's the beauty of it. You don't compete against anyone else, only against yourself. And you can always beat your previous performance, so weight lifting is a perfect way to build your confidence in yourself as a winner. Celebrate your achievements. Enjoy!

If you're a newcomer to weight lifting, be sure to start slowly. The first time out, you'll probably be able to lift more weight than your body can really handle. If you aren't very restrained in your first workout, you may become painfully stiff a few hours later. Start slowly. If you don't have a friend who works out and have never been in a gym, phone several gyms first. Ask whether you have to sign a contract that can't be cancelled by you. The better gyms allow you to cancel on thirty days' notice. Ask about their enrollment fees. Then walk into the gym dressed for a workout and you're sure to find a very helpful trainer who'll get you started.

But remember, the trainer may have been lifting weights for so long that he or she has forgotten what it is to be a couch potato. Don't let them push you too hard to begin with.

The most important thing is to adjust your attitude so that you take pleasure in feeling your body toughen. Never let yourself think that working out is drudgery; you can make it fun if you look at it right.

Running Versus Walking

It's largely a function of age. If you're under forty and not badly overweight, you'll probably prefer running to walking once you're ready for it. Work up to a brisk two miles a day walk, and continue to hold off on running until you just can't stand to keep on walking.

If you're on the wise side of forty, consider sticking with walking for the rest of your life. Walking gives your bones and joints far less grief than running.

Do What You Enjoy

The vital thing is to train yourself to like your healthy new lifestyle. People who stop smoking are often amazed at smelling tobacco on themselves for weeks after they give up the coffin nails. It takes time for all the tar to work its way out of your body. Enjoy that tobacco fragrance? It's a sure sign that you've taken command of your health and longevity.

In your choice of exercise, choose what you enjoy. Different areas offer different choices, but you can bike or walk almost any place outside of the larger cities. Vary your street walks with hikes in the country. Find a public pool you can swim in. Play tennis or racquetball.

Golf is recreation, pure and simple; its exercise value is zero. You can't even walk from tee to tee; you have to ride. Play golf if you enjoy it, but get your exercise some other way.

Eat to Stay Alive

Get a cholesterol profile and have it explained to you. If your doctor won't do this, find another doctor, because being ignorant of your cholesterol is life-threatening. It's your life I'm talking about.

Your cholesterol profile will consist of several numbers:

1. **Total cholesterol.** In recent years, doctors have been saying that anything under 200 is good, but this is not low enough to eliminate heart attack risk, recent research has proven.
2. **HDL** (the "good cholesterol"). The higher the better.
3. **LDL** (the "bad cholesterol"). The lower the better.
4. **Triglycerides.** The lower the better.
5. An important element in your cholesterol profile is the **ratio** of the various components to each other. Have your doctor explain what the ideal ratios are, and the implications of where your profile falls.

If the numbers and your doctor tell you that you're at risk of heart attack, get busy with changing your lifestyle (eating, smoking, drinking, and exercise habits). The life you save will be your own.

Yes, eat to stay alive. Food is essential, but if your primary consideration in choosing what you eat is taste and the pleasure it gives you, start giving serious consideration to revising your thinking. Taste can still come first, but now that the food industry is providing more healthy food than was available just five years ago, you can make nutrition a close second in importance.

Proverbs 8:11
"For wisdom is better than rubies; and all the things that may be
desired are not to be compared to it."

CHAPTER 4
Build Your Mental Discipline

The Goal Is to Automatically Focus on Opportunities rather Than on Obstacles

It's surprising how easy it is to fall into the habit of seeing problems and risks in every challenge and blinding us to the opportunities it offers. By definition, change opens new doors; it doesn't only close old ones. If you choose to see only the closed doors, you condemn yourself to be battered by change, not helped to achieve new things.

Consider some of the changes that have hit what was called, for a time, "the rust belt." Many cities there were hammered by the sudden decline of their essential industries. The accompanying loss of payrolls devastated the local retail trades and professions. Today, most of those cities are thriving; their reeducated workforces have good and often better jobs in newer companies that are attuned to the new information age.

Of course, this renaissance has been uneven. Some areas have been slow to completely throw off the economic disasters caused by their failures to meet the challenges of change in new ways. And even in the most progressive cities, many individuals couldn't adapt to new ways and will never be as well off as formerly. The price of change is high; the price of blindly fighting change is even higher.

When faced by the onslaught of change in your field, don't put off taking action to get yourself ready to adapt. Remember: it's always later than you think.

Discipline Is a Do-It-Yourself Training Regime

Training yourself to have more mental discipline is the least understood and most important skill known to humankind. Mental discipline—without it, we accomplish nothing. With it, there are no limits to what we can do.

Here's an important but little-known fact: your emotions and your mind can be trained in the same basic way that you would train yourself to have greater physical capacity. No, I'm not saying that the best way to increase your mental discipline is with athletic exercises, although working out regularly calls for a high degree of mental discipline.

Mental discipline does not exist in a vacuum. It comes from having clear goals that are designed with emotional intensity. Set your goals on achievements that you greatly desire. No goal is too great to be effective in giving you mental discipline as long as you truly believe you can achieve it within the limits imposed by your patience and resolve.

If you know in your heart that you can't achieve something, it can't be a goal. That something can only be a wish, a daydream, and a fantasy. Wishing upon a star won't make you a pilot; setting up a realistic plan for gaining the necessary skills and accreditation will give you wings.

Set goals that lie just beyond your easy grasp. You want a challenge (make it harder), but you also want to build on wins (make it easier). Work out a compromise between those two extremes so you will achieve the first goal and then have greater confidence to conquer the next, higher goal.

If you feel you lack discipline, that is, if you feel you lack the drive to actually do what you want to do, you are like a couch potato who wants to run a marathon. You have a long way to go, and if you try to run the marathon on the first day, you won't make it. It's the same with discipline training.

Set small tasks for yourself in the three areas of life: emotional, physical, and mental. As much as you can, connect these small tasks with goals you want to accomplish and things you like to do. If you find that you get a little tense playing certain video games, you might add a brief daily session with the game that causes you the most tension. Over time, the tension will decrease as you gain greater confidence and skill at the game. This will increase your ability to function effectively under emotional pressure.

Setting up exercises to increase your physical capacity is easy. Any physical activity that can be measured will do, if repeated regularly. Setting up exercises to increase your mental capacity is only more difficult because most people have no experience doing so. Abraham Lincoln mastered Euclid's geometry, not because he had any interest in geometry, but because he wanted to train his mind.

Today, we choose among an almost limitless number of mental challenges to expand our mental capacities. Learn a new language, master calculus, become a better chess player, memorize poetry, expand your vocabulary, develop your computer skills further. Master any new technology that will increase your earning power or personal convenience and pleasure. Learn how to repair your car. Setting specific goals in any of these areas—and following through until you have achieved your goal and mastered the desired benefit—is a powerful way to increase your discipline.

Keep doing it. Spend more of your time on self-improvement and less on self-entertainment (via the boob tube). In other words, instead of watching other people play all the time, get in there and play the game yourself. The richness of your life isn't measured by how many hours you spend watching other people perform, but on how many hours you spend perfecting your own performance.

Mental Challenge: The Importance of Lifelong Exercise for the Mind

Some people think that education stops when they leave class. Since all the book learning they have acquired came from sitting in a classroom, it never occurs to them to learn on their own when they leave school.

However, the true function of education below the college level is to provide you with the skills to learn more on your own, following your personal desires and interests. Devote at least an hour of each day to learning new things about your career and the world. This is probably the most important hour of your day; use it well.

Create and Grow Rich Mentally

Anyone with a creative idea put into enthusiastic action is preparing society for the future. The more you open your mind and rid yourself of the garbage we've allowed to be put into our craniums, the sooner we'll discover our strengths and positive qualities that will enable us to reach our fullest potentials. I call this slow process "creatalating" (create a late ing). Yes, it's a new word I coined. It merely means we know what is right for us. When this is accomplished and others notice, they often call it genius.

When I wrote my first book, *Argument with an Angel*, I believe thoughts were coming from above, giving me knowledge of the past and present, and laying plans that, one day, we would have a more peaceful world. Yes, it is a fairy tale. Since the publication of this book, many more ideas for books, tapes, articles, paintings, and other inspirational products that I believe will one day benefit society have been filling my mind. My mind was like a tornado or hurricane, and when the eye of the storm left things in shambles, I was able to sift through and simplify life. As a result, I developed my audiotape: "The Success Equation for Life."

Keep your mind busy. It seems that my mind is always in a state of motion, even when I'm asleep.

Asking questions is what will give you the results and answers you want. Often while sleeping, dozing, napping, opening a book, running into a stranger, or working on a new project, you will receive the answers you need for your new invention, book, poem, song, painting, or other creative projects.

CHAPTER 5

Multiply Your Creativity with Spiritual Power

It seems that everyone tries to tell me what I am. My mother always asked why I couldn't be like other kids. Others called me dumb shit. It took me years to learn to overcome those early traumas. I hate labels.

The Goal Is a Joyful, Giving Lifestyle in a Gimmie World

Because you're overweight, people call you fat and make fun of you. Because of all the labels, I learned to love solitude. Possibly, this is why I now excel in some of the areas that require solitude. In this silent time, I learned to write, paint, draw, and speak. I learned that I was not as dysfunctional as everyone said I was.

Spiritual Power Comes at a Price

I've felt misplaced much of my life. In my early years, I was labeled a slow learner and put in remedial classes. I just prayed to be good at something one day. So I started talking to imaginary characters and leaders of the past and present, asking for assistance so I wouldn't feel so stupid. Even after some of my accomplishments, I'm still being labeled. Some of the churches are now calling me a New Ager. In my mind, I'm just a Christian. It seems that everyone is trying to tell me what I am.

So far, I get happier the older I get. I was an old man when I was young. By living your dreams, it makes you more creative and forces you to use your mental capacity continually, elevating you to new possibilities of thinking. By going through this process, there are many failures, but this is the way we learn.

Make an Ongoing Commitment to Spiritual Power

I love to create and try to develop things that will better people's lives. Why can't people see that all learning is interrelated? If you have a need, try and find solutions for them.

We learn by failing. I have learned that if you help enough people with their needs, they will give you your wants, so use your mental capacity to the fullest, for it can help you to *create* and *grow rich*.

CHAPTER 6
Financial Happiness

What Would It Take to Make You Financially Happy?

"**M**ore" is probably closest to the truth for most of us. If we set a figure and reach it, chances are we'll want more. But an unremitting drive for more, more, and even more is likely to destroy rather than build happiness.

Balance is the key to success. On one side is money-getting, that is, work. On the other side are all the finer things life offers for your enjoyment, that is, play. Maintain a rough balance between work and play or you'll miss out on the best life has to offer. You can never live this day, this hour, this minute again. Keep firmly in mind that life is not a rehearsal. Enjoying life is a do-it-yourself project; in fact, it's our most important project.

The Goal Is Fiscal Freedom, Not Merely the Avoidance of Bankruptcy

Fiscal freedom is when you have enough resources to live on a level you consider comfortable and do what you want without working. Anything less than that is the mere avoidance of bankruptcy. The only way anyone ever reaches fiscal freedom is by paying the price for it.

Financial Success Has Its Own Price

Many of us tend to run our lives constantly on the edge of financial disaster, never building financial security through the accumulation of investment capital. Why don't we? We all know the power of compound interest over time.

We don't accumulate because we want it now. The slow accumulation of investment capital isn't as gratifying as whatever we spend money on. Changing this attitude is another exercise in mental discipline. Do I say it's easy? No, it's not. For most of us, it's very hard.

Set Your Goals Right

What we need is a set of financial goals that excites us. Some people are inspired to great sacrifices and exertions simply by greed to have more. However, most of us need to connect our financial goals with rewards. We don't crave money for itself; we want what money can buy. Certainly, this is a healthier attitude than greed for greed's sake.

Begin saving whatever figure you feel comfortable with, but begin. As you see your money grow, it will inspire you to continue and possibly increase your rate of savings. The vital thing is to begin.

It has often been said that you should pay yourself along with paying all the other bills. Paying yourself, of course, means saving the money. Start with a percentage of your income. Ten percent is a popular figure. Select a number you can stay with long enough for the habit to become firmly rooted in your personality.

Money, the Tool

As previously stated, a healthy attitude toward money is essential to success.

You've heard the negative clichés, such as, "Money can't buy happiness" and "Money is the root of all evil."

The fact is, money is the single most important element of society today, and if used properly, money is good. Remember, though, that money is a tool, not a goal. Money is a means to an end, not an end to the means. If you use money for good, you will likely avoid the pitfalls that so many confused people have fallen into.

A few examples include:

Charles Schwab – former president of a large steel company, who died indebted.

Richard Whitney – a previous president of the New York Stock Exchange, who spent time in prison.

Albert Fall – a past member of the president's cabinet, who was pardoned from prison to die at home.

Jesse Livermore – once the biggest man on Wall Street, who committed suicide.

There are many more, but these are enough to illustrate my point.

The sad truth is that in the twelve years or more that we attend school, we are taught a wide range of skills, but not how to make money, much less how to keep it or grow with it. I'm going to touch on a few of the basics, which should serve as a guide for the success of your financial future.

First, we'll address budgeting. Yes, it is painful when you're starting out, but it is essential if you want to be in control of your spending habits. You have to walk before you can run, so we'll start by finding out where you are, so you'll know where you can go from there. Be as accurate as possible. This should reflect reality, not wishful thinking.

Dr. Jan Cooper

What Is Your Financial Worth?														
Cash and Bank Accounts														
Surrender Value of Life Insurance														
Cash-In Value of Savings Bonds														
Stocks, Mutual Funds														
Cash-In Value of Retirement Funds														
Commissions and Fees Due														
Income Tax Refunds														
Real Property														
Cars														
Boats, Recreation Vehicles														
Machines, Tools, Equipment														
Furniture, Appliances														
Silver, Crystal, and China														
Jewelry and Furs														
Coin Collections														
Stamp Collections														
Personal Business Equity														
Equity in Trust or Estates														
Other Assets														
Your Total Worth														

What Is Your Hard-Earned Cash Going?																
Total Monthly Income (Take-Home Pay)																
Expenses																
Groceries and Bakery																
Vegetables and Fruit																
Meat, Fish, Poultry																
Dairy																
Lunches																
Restaurant																
Snacks, Etc.																
Total Food Expense																
House Payment or Rent (tax and ins.)																
Gas																
Electricity																
Water and Sewer																
Garbage																
Phone																
House and Yard Maintenance																
Cleaning Supplies, Etc.																
Personal Care Items																
Total Home Upkeep Expense																
Health Insurance																
Doctor Bills																
Medicines																
Total Medical Expense																
Car Payments																
Auto Repairs																
Insurance, Parking, Etc.																
Total Auto Expense																

Tickets (Movies, Sports, Etc.)											
Tobacco, Beverages, Etc.											
Hobbies											
Vacation											
Total Recreation Expense											
Education Fees											
Magazines, Etc.											
Lessons											
Total Education Expense											
Church											
Charities											
Total Contributions Expense											
Miscellaneous											
Total Monthly Expense											

Your Monthly Budget

Education	Transport	Material	Business	Promo

Recreation																						
Medical																						
Personal																						
Clothes																						
Food																						

Home	Care																											
Housing	Upkeep																											
Savings	10%																											
Date																												

There is some disagreement as to how one should go about filling out the forms. I recommend that when filling out the form concerning your total worth, you use the value that you could get out of the items if you had to liquidate tomorrow. Some believe that the better idea is to use the replacement values. Maybe you could try both. You'd be surprised at the broadness of the spectrum.

Now that you are aware of your net worth and your approximate monthly outgo, try budgeting. Write down your expected expenses for the month in each category. Then daily write down your actual expense in each area. At the end of the month, total each category and compare those with your projected expectations.

If you follow this format, you will achieve financial success. If you are just throwing money away, you will know it. After a month or two, you will also know where to make adjustments in your spending.

I suggest that you make at least a dozen copies of the last form regarding budgeting. My goal here is to make it so much a part of your life that you will continue to budget from now on. You'll find that you will save money.

As you can see, the 10% savings is listed in the first column. There is a reason for this. I have found that when trying to save if that money does not come out first, at the end of the month, there is nothing left to save. Another way of looking at it is "Pay yourself first." Now, doesn't that make sense?

Let's assume that you make only a pitiful $500.00 a month. Ten percent of that is only $50.00, which, I assure you, would disappear into the unknown anyway, so let's put it to work. If you were to put $50.00 a month under your mattress, after a period of five years, you would have $3,000. Based on simple interest of six percent over the same period of time, you would gain an additional $585.20. That is nearly twenty percent more.

1st	Year	600.00	36.00	636,00
2nd	Year	1,236.00	74.16	1,310.16
3rd	Year	1,910.16	114.61	2,024.77
4th	Year	2,624.77	157.49	2,782.26
5th	Year	3,382.26	202.94	3,585.20

Keep in mind that this small sample is based only on simple interest.

You might be interested to know exactly how much your time is worth. Wasted time is worthless time.

Year	Day	Hour	Minute
$10,000	41.67	5.21	.09
$15,000	62.50	7.81	.13
$20,000	83.34	10.42	.17
30,000	125.00	15.00	.25

We don't need to go any further to illustrate my point. I just thought you might find it interesting

Proverbs 16:6
"By mercy and truth iniquity is purged: and by the fear of the Lord men depart from evil."

CHAPTER 7
Blend Your Lifestyle into Joyful Living

Your Goal Is a Life Filled with Emotional Rewards

Although many of the greatest emotional rewards are free, many of us are so preoccupied that we fail to appreciate them. Enjoying life's free emotional rewards is a living skill; like all skills, it can be learned and developed. Rate yourself on the five-scale for your intensity of enjoyment of some of these free emotional rewards:

Laughter

Do you work at putting more laughter into your life? It's nature's greatest healer and, next to sound sleep, the greatest tonic for tired minds and bodies.

If you need more laughter in your daily routine (and who doesn't?), program it in. Here are a few ways:

1. **TV** probably has more funny stuff than you watch now. If so, program your VCR to record the comedy channels and sitcoms, and at least the monologues on late-night shows.
2. **Collect videos** of movie comedies. Play one of them when you need a good shot of laughter.
3. **Collect comedy audiocassettes**. Play one while driving to work and arrive there in an upbeat frame of mind.
4. **Collect jokes**, and relate them often.
5. **Seek out companions who love to laugh**.

6. **Study humor**. Some of the basic methods of tickling the funny bone are well known.
7. **Use the Internet** to gather jokes from online friends.

One day, two cats were sitting by a tennis court, watching the ball bounce back and forth over the net. "Hey," exclaimed the first cat, "I didn't know you liked to watch tennis."

"Actually, I don't," responded the other cat. "The only reason I'm remotely interested is because my father's in the racket."

Yes, even jokes or humorous stories are products. This joke is contributed by E.H. Cole. Remember to release your creative genius.

Nature

Intensify your love of our planet.

Since the grandeur of nature is so incredibly diverse and widespread, no matter where we live, we must travel to view most of it. Probably, no one lives long enough to see everything the planet has to offer: all of the waterfalls, active volcanoes and geysers, forests, majestic mountains, scenic rivers, fantastic canyons and fjords, delightful islands, coral reefs, and wildlife in their natural habitats.

But not all of nature's grandeur is far away. Make time to admire the splendor of sunsets or dawns and the ever-changing panorama of clouds visible from the deepest concrete canyon. At night, get to a backyard or rooftop, or an open space away from lights, and enjoy the star-studded sky.

Learn to appreciate nature's splendors more intensely—few activities can enrich your life more.

Family

Our loved ones are our anchors, keeping us safely moored against every hurricane of life. Never miss a chance to strengthen your family's ties with each other. Treasure your mental snapshots of joyful moments.

Participate in Sports

It's far better to be the guy who couldn't finish the 10K race than the potato who won't get off the couch except to look for the remote or refill the chip bowl. Find a sport you enjoy that's within your physical capabilities, and *play.*

Watching Professional Sports

Drinking to the extent of damaging personal relationships is a classic symptom of alcohol addiction. Watching professional sports can also damage personal relationships, as many self-proclaimed football widows will testify. Sports addicts need the excitement that watching professional teams provides, but, unlike participatory sports, its exercise value is nil. If you are serious about achieving your goals, rather than watching professional athletes achieve theirs, curb your sports addiction.

Giving Compliments

Being able to praise others with sincerity and warmth builds personal happiness. Make a habit of it.

Receiving Compliments

The quantity and quality of the compliments you get usually depends on the quantity and quality of the compliments you give others.

Exercise Highs

Marathoners tell of the highs they get from running. Whether or not this causes addiction is debatable. However, marathoners include a higher percentage of former alcoholics than is found among the general population.

Strongly motivating highs can be obtained more easily from many other kinds of exercise. If you need more spice in your life, try getting it from exercise, so you benefit in two ways.

Taste

Thin people probably enjoy food as much as thick people do. The difference is that thinnies have mastered the art of training down to appreciate low-fat foods. You can do it, too. It's easy—just take it a little at a time. And, as an extra bonus, you'll get an emotional reward from every pound you drop. Just remember one thing: diet alone doesn't cause weight loss; you need exercise, too.

Music

Music can be soothing or stimulating and, by enhancing any mood, it can deliver emotional rewards throughout the day and evening. Harness its power to increase your pleasure at play and your work performance on the job. Use headphones if necessary to avoid disturbing others.

Reading

Add depth and excitement to your emotional rewards by exploring the world's great minds. They're all there for free in any public library.

TV

If the TV is always on at your house, the chances are that most of the brains there are turned off most of the time. TV, one of the twentieth century's greatest plagues, has followed us into the new millennium with increased virulence. Addiction to TV may be today's greatest block to personal achievement, being more widespread than drug or alcohol addiction. If you're addicted, get a life! Get on with pursuing your goals. The TV will still be there when you're too old to do anything except watch it.

How to Enjoy Your Work, Whatever It Is

1. Concentrate on doing it better—and with a cheerful word and smile for everyone you encounter. I realize that this suggestion will seem unrealistic in some situations, but unless your occupation is going underground to clean sewers, you can probably enjoy your work more if you make an effort to do it better, and more cheerfully.
2. Figure out ways to make yourself more useful to your bosses. If you're self-employed, your clients and customers are your bosses.
3. Work toward a goal. That is, regard your work as a stepping stone to a better-paying and more satisfying position. Looking ahead can make it easier to overlook small irritations because you're not going to be there forever—you're moving up soon, right?
4. Set yourself a personal goal to do your work so superlatively well and with such warm cheerfulness that you surprise many of the people you meet during work hours. It's a lot more fun than merely wishing the time would pass quicker.

Joyful Living Is Disciplined Living

Most people live carelessly without goals—without the constant discipline that having a specific plan imposes. Lacking goals, they have condemned themselves to wander aimlessly. On the other hand, when you have clearly defined goals, you have reasons to make and carry out positive decisions. You know what you want and what you don't want. You can stay focused on your goals and achieve them, unlike goal-deprived people who can't.

Job 28: 18
"No mention shall be made of coral, or of pearls: for the price
of wisdom is above rubies."

CHAPTER 8
Design Your Own Success Profile

The first step is to decide precisely what success is for you. It doesn't work to simply think about it. To power your drive to achieve your goals, write all their specifics down. Why? For three reasons: (I) because writing your success goals down helps you to be very specific about them, (II) detailing them on paper helps you visualize them more vividly, and (III) clarifying your choices on paper helps you eliminate conflicts between them and makes them practical.

In other words, go into great detail. Write down what you would consider as being a state of success for you—not for somebody else but for you. Do this in terms of what you have achieved, and are achieving, with your life. Jot down what your position will be. Give a clear description of where you would be living, what investments and other things you would own, the car you would be driving, and the recreational facilities you'd be enjoying. Decide between a yacht and a Windsurfer, a vacation home or an RV, a hang glider or an airplane. List every place in the world you want to visit, and be specific about any other achievements that are important to you.

If you don't know exactly what success is for you, how will you know when you get there? Just as important, are you as strongly motivated to achieve your vision of success as you could be? If not, detail your goals on paper so you can use the power of visualization more effectively to get you where you want to go.

Why Do People Self-Destruct?

Any self-defeating behavior keeps people from reaching their goals. Many people do things that are not in their own best interest. I know because I've done many things that were not in my best interest, as we all have.

Procrastination is only a problem with me if it is something I don't want to do. The things I don't like doing and tend to put off, I now hire someone to complete, giving me the time to do what I'm best at.

Some self-destruct because of attitudes, behavior, habits, talking too much, not listening, having to be right all the time, being argumentative, and not accepting people as they are. There are too many causes of self-destruction for me to go into each of them in detail.

Instead, let's talk about the most important aspect of self-destruction: how do we stop our self-destructive behavior?

Ask yourself, "If I could start all over, what would I do differently?" List all of your responses. Then every time you are tempted to do that same dumb thing, read over all the reasons you would love to have another chance to start over. Start looking at your choices from the physical and mental health standpoint; consider their effect on you spiritually, and financially.

If you put your self-destruction stopper plan into action by listing all of your major mistakes and asking for a chance to correct each of them for written reasons, you will not self-destruct. It's your decision.

But since you're reading this book, you will certainly turn away from anything like self-destruction and throw your energies into achieving great things. You have ideas, plans, and inventions that can improve yourself or the world. Start now to make them realities.

Being an artist the majority of my life, I love what Michelangelo said: "The greater danger for most of us is not that our aim is too high and we miss it, but it is too low and we reach it." So stretch yourself, so you have the opportunity to reach your highest potential.

Ben Franklin wrote: "'Tis easier to prevent bad habits than to break them." If only I had listened and learned from his experiences, I could be further ahead. This applies to all of us.

Will Rogers was like dynamite. Listen to what he once said: "Even if you are on the right track, you will get run over if you just sit there."

You must let people know you exist. You must promote. You must advertise. You must be honest. People cannot buy from you if they don't know you exist. You know what you should do. You know where to start. You have all the answers to your problems. Just remember to keep a journal, to be curious about all things, to write down your beliefs so you can learn from yourself and your experiences. Your behavior today determines your future.

Once you have stretched your mind, it can never return to its original state. A friend of mine, Barbara Winter, said, "Your fantasy can only be what it wants you to be." I gather from this that it is your imagination that determines your outcome.

Aristotle said, "Where your talents and the world's needs cross, there lies your vocation."

So please, don't self-destruct—the world needs you.

Master the Art of Self-Reconstruction

Here are the five key concepts for reconstructing yourself, whether it is physical, mental, emotional, or spiritual.

Be Persistent

Nothing worth accomplishing can be done unless it is pursued with determination.

Work Incrementally

Break overwhelmingly large tasks into small chunks you can pick up and run with. If faced with a challenge too great for your present strength, skill, or knowledge, find ways to increase your potential until you can meet and beat the challenge.

Have Faith in Yourself

Give yourself every possible break by preparing for challenges as thoroughly as possible, and then go forward with complete confidence.

Reward Yourself for Progress

Compliment others on their progress; reward yourself for your own progress in nondestructive ways.

Affirm Your Success

Visualizing your goal as already being achieved is a powerful spur to its accomplishment.

CHAPTER 9
Smooth Paths to Swift Success

I s the path to success ever smooth? Our answer comes from the Oval Office: "It depends on how you define smooth." Our own definition might change over time. The path might seem rough as we go over it, but looking back, we often realize that it was really quite smooth.

Compile Your Accomplishments List

A human tendency is to remember the hurts, failures, and embarrassments we all experience as we go through life. Curiously, we don't need to list them because we never forget a single one. Our accomplishments and successes tend to drift out of our memory because, often, no great emotion was involved. Have you ever had the experience of having someone tell you about something fine you said or did once? They remembered, but you didn't until they reminded you.

Forgetting our accomplishments is a careless waste of one of our most precious assets. Compile a list of your accomplishments. Review it to build your confidence when you face a difficult challenge. Review that list to restore your confidence and good feelings after taking some sort of an emotional hit. You'll be glad you did.

Develop a Way to Please the Buying Public

People who have pleased the buying public have done so in many different ways, but their output shares one readily identifiable quality—highly distinctive style. We hear a single note and know it's

Streisand, a glimpse at a painting tells us it's a Picasso, one shot of a building reveals that we're looking at another of Frank Lloyd Wright's masterpieces.

Only rarely is creating and refining a highly distinctive style easy. Most of us have to study long and labor hard to develop it, but once it's working, it's yours forever. If you're active in a field that's popular with the buying public, having a highly distinctive style will multiply the benefits you receive from your work enormously.

Become Highly Visible in the Community

The "community" might be the area where you live, where you work, or it might be the community of individuals who are doing what you're doing, your *career community*. In many cases, your career community will be divided into two parts: (a) your colleagues, as just mentioned, and (b) the people who buy, use, or appreciate what you produce in the widest sense of the word. If you're a poet, you produce poems; if a singer, songs; if a painter, you produce paintings. If you're a singer, your career community is the total group of other singers, wherever they happen to be at the moment. If you're an artist, every art gallery and colony in the world is part of your career community.

While your main effort at making yourself more visible in your community should target your career community, don't overlook the value of being well known in your hometown. As your accomplishments grow, publicize yourself locally. Many benefits flow from localized publicity.

Perfect a Vibrant Schedule of Success: Create, Promote, and Play

Aim to spend about a third of your time creating, a third promoting your creations, and a third rewarding yourself with play. In the beginning of your career, the last will get less time at the end; the first two will take less. The vital thing is to schedule adequate play as soon as financial realities permit. Why is adequate play vital?

It's often called "recharging the battery" because this metaphor is so vivid. The effort level you are capable of—both in strength and quality—depends entirely on the energy you have stored in your mind and body—just as you depend on the electrical energy stored in your car's battery to start it. If your car's generator fails and isn't repaired, the time will soon come when you can't start your car.

In exactly the same way, if you don't replace the energy drained from your energy stores by work and all the processes of living, the time will come when your gears won't grind out your finest work. They may not even turn at all. Burnout destroys creativity. Recharge your batteries regularly with nutritious food, sound sleep, and time off spent in activities unrelated to your work.

Ecclesiastes 7:12
"For wisdom is a defence, and money is a defence: but the excellency of knowledge is, that wisdom giveth life to them that have it."

Part Two
Your Right Wing—Selling

E verybody sells. Politicians must sell their ideas; all professionals must sell their services, even though many of them seem to do so indirectly. Parents endeavor to sell their values to their children—I could go on.

My Success Equation is of great value in enhancing your Selling Success. Here it is again.

$$TCFWY = HW + T + N + M + AQ + S + H + 7S \times PPP^2 \times P^{10}$$

Now let's talk about the nuts and bolts of successful selling. Start off by resolving to invest heavily—using more time and energy than cash—in enhancing your methods and skills at selling your capabilities, concepts, and creativity. This part of the book is chockfull of ideas to help you do this.

Psalm 112:1,3
"Blessed is the man that feareth the Lord,
that delighteth greatly in His commandments...
Wealth and riches shall be in his house."

CHAPTER 10

Turn the Spotlight on Yourself with Adroit Publicity

Establish Yourself as the Authority in Your Niche

How do you establish yourself as an authority? It's quite simple in theory. You simply start telling the world that you are the authority.

Here Are Five Ways to Do This:

1. **Write and publish** the strongest book you can, and then tell the world that it's the best ever in your niche.
2. Give seminars at The Learning Annex and similar training facilities. You won't clear much money by doing this, but you're mainly there for the exposure. The most valuable part of which is the ad for you and your seminar they'll put in the catalog they mail in huge numbers.
3. **Tape one of your seminars.** Have a cassette duplication shop run off a batch of single cassettes—or an album if you have enough material. Sell these at your seminars.
4. **Write a newspaper column.** Most areas have local weekly newspapers of the kind you see stacked in racks in coffee shops that are free for the taking. Being supported entirely by advertising, their budgets are tight, so don't expect payment for your column. Remember, it still has to be well written, delivered regularly, on time, and on a subject of interest to their readers.

5. **Syndicate your column** yourself—visit your local library and get a directory of newspapers across the country that are likely to use your column, and start sending it to them.

Exploit Existing Channels for Maximum Free Publicity

America's news media has an enormous amount of space and time to fill every day. They jump quickest on "hard news"—murders, hurricanes, scandals are among the high and mighty. But there's never enough hard news, so they're always hungry for stuff to fill their space. What they want is something new and exciting, or a new twist on something old and exciting. Supply such a subject and they'll run with it, and this will give you and what you do a huge amount of exposure. The existing channels, although created and maintained at great expense, will give you free exposure if you have the right message.

Exposure through Electronic Media

Phone the shows that cover your general area of interest when you're ready to deliver a ten-second pitch that excites the interest of the producers. Also, be ready to send follow-up materials—your book, for example, when requested. Look into the possibility of being featured on TV talk shows and radio talk shows as well.

Exposure through Print Media

As mentioned before, submit articles to newspapers, magazines, and newsletters that cover topics related to your field of expertise.

Invest Wisely Where You'll Get the Most Publicity Bang for Your Bucks

Digital Opportunities

The Internet is evolving rapidly. Use your access to the World Wide Web to search for the areas where you can make the most impact *today* with your message.

Here's a place to start: on the Alta Vista Search Engine, search for *Directories*. Lots of stuff will come up, and you can go from there. Many of the best directories of newspapers and broadcast media are available on CD or even online.

A Web site for your seminar can be set up at very low cost or even for free, but be sure to check free offers carefully. Sometimes, they involve long-term commitments.

Once your Web site is ready for visitors and you have something specific to promote or sell, begin visiting chat rooms that discuss your subject and start posting messages. Some of them restrict commercial messages, so plan a subtle approach.

Print Opportunities

The Yearbook of Experts, Authorities & Spokespersons® accepts advertisements. A small investment here gives you a lot of exposure and credibility. You can contact them at: www.yearbooknews.com.

Sharing Ideas News Magazine is loaded with helpful information for speakers. If you give seminars, you must have this magazine. You can contact Dottie Walters, publisher, at: www.waltersintl.com.

Become Your Own Publicity Manager

Good PR people don't come cheap. They start at four-figure retainers payable *every month.* So, at first, you may have no choice but to manage your own publicity. Books and workshops offer a great deal of information about the fascinating subject of publicity. A good place to start is *The Publicity Handbook* by David R. Yale.

Create Striking Promotional Materials

Boring promotional materials achieve boring results. Get the best help you can afford and put out beautiful materials. Use full color (four-color process) if possible. It's so commonplace today that black ink on white paper isn't impressive. Fancy dye-cuts are expensive and probably not worth the money. Test your ideas in the marketplace before you print huge quantities.

Give Talks to Church and Civic Groups

The program chairperson at most church and civic groups (Lions Club, Rotary Club, and so on) are always on the hunt for good speakers. Their budget for speaker fees is generally zero, but it's excellent practice and exposure.

Set Publicity Goals

Wait until you have tested the waters and have some clear insights into what's involved, and then start setting publicity goals. This is a vital part of the planning I talked about in Part One.

The large companies may or may not be able to afford this sloppiness, but the small operator can't. Study this question carefully, and focus your follow-up on the decision-makers in your area of interest.

Stage Events

You can lower or even eliminate your expense of staging an event by lining up a sponsor. A doctor who specializes in longevity decided to promote his practice by giving seminars to the general public, but was deterred by the costs involved. He looked over the products he was recommending, and contacted one of the manufacturers. They were happy to pick up the meeting room rental and the advertising cost of promoting his seminars in return for a brief favorable mention of their product and the discreet display of their logos and product literature.

Did this sort of promotion do the drug manufacturer any good? Who knows? But it helped the doctor enormously.

Join the Right Organizations

The local chapters of an amazing variety of organizations are found in most cities. Study what's available within an easy distance of your home. Attend meetings as a guest to get a firsthand impression of how belonging to the organization can help you achieve your goals. For an invitation, call the membership chairperson.

For maximum benefit from membership in any group, get involved. If you're willing to work, you'll quickly find yourself elected to office in the chapter. The key to all this is to choose carefully, so that your available time is spent where it will give you the greatest results.

Issue Press Releases

Build your list of people to get your press releases before you start writing them because creating the list can be time consuming. Then, when you have at least twenty people on your list, start sending them press releases every time you do something, such as being selected as a speaker somewhere, having your book published, making an appearance on a radio or TV show, or inventing something new.

How large should your press release list be? Computerize it so you can machine-select the most likely people to read and use each of your press releases. If you do this, your list can't be too large. However, unless you can machine-select the best recipients for each press release or other mailing, everybody gets everything. This is destructive in two ways: (a) it costs too much; (b) it trains recipients to trash your messages without reading them.

Hold Press Conferences

If you can write a credible press release, you can hold a press conference. However, it's advisable to use discretion here, and only call in the press when you have something newsworthy to report. Hold it in a convenient location and provide suitable refreshments.

CHAPTER 11

Boost Your Products/Services and Yourself with Efficient Advertising

Advertising has to be efficient or it will drag you under. Your advertising has to bring in more than enough new business to pay for itself. Many years ago, one of America's most successful merchants—a heavy advertiser—said, "Half my advertising is pure waste. Unfortunately, I don't know which half." It's an old complaint.

Looking at advertising from a different perspective, more than two centuries ago, Samuel Johnson wrote: "Advertisements are now so numerous that they are very negligently perused, and it is therefore necessary to gain attention by magnificence of promises, and by eloquences sometimes sublime and sometimes pathetic."

Things have gone downhill since Johnson grumbled about the state of advertising in 1758. It's estimated that up to ninety-eight percent of advertising expenditures don't pay their way.

Consider the print ads and TV commercials created by large ad agencies. Many of them leave you in the dark as to what's being advertised—which, clearly, is a tremendous waste of money. Giant corporations can afford to flush their ad budgets down the toilet, but I can't. Can you?

Effective advertising isn't expensive. In fact, it's one of your most profitable investments—because it's in yourself.

Make Your Advertising Dollars Pay Off—Always Track Response

Put most of your effort and money into publicity because you get a lot more bang for the buck. However, in some situations, there's no substitute for paid advertising. Consider your ad options carefully, and lean toward those that allow you to determine results. In fact, I'll go further and urge you to avoid any advertising medium where results cannot be known.

It usually requires ingenuity, but there are often ways to measure how effective your advertising is. Unless you can determine whether your paid advertising is doing the intended job, you're probably throwing your advertising money away.

Test, Test, Test

Direct mail advertising lends itself to testing different offers, but old hands know that you can only test one variable at a time. The identical offer mailed on different days of the week may produce vastly different results. Merely changing the color or size of the envelope can change results. So testing isn't easy. But it's essential if you want to improve overall returns.

Write Copy that Really Sells

First, define exactly what you want the ad to accomplish, then eliminate everything that doesn't further that goal.

Tips on Writing Selling Copy

It's basically common sense, something lacking to a startling degree in most advertising done by large companies and by smaller operations, too. Here are nine tips for writing stronger ad copy, or for analyzing an ad copy that someone else writes for you.

1. Use the 80/20 Rule

Devote fourth-fifths of your ad to telling the readers how they will benefit from your product/service, and only one-fifth to telling how great you are. The point is that they don't care how great you are unless you have something of benefit to them.

2. Announce What You're Selling Up Front

Third-rate ad agencies—the ones that lack an understanding of the basic purpose of advertising—love to come up with print ads and TV commercials that are long on cuteness but painfully short on selling power. Usually, they leave the casual viewer completely in the dark as to what's being advertised. If you're offered such an ad, fire the agency instantly and head for the nearest exit.

3. Tell Them How To Contact You

It's incredible, but many ads either hide or omit how and where the product/service can be bought. Apparently, such advertisers are convinced that their prospective buyers will go to great pains to find them; it's the sort of arrogance that leads to massive failure.

4. Use Ordinary English Words

When writing ads, never forget for an instant what Samuel Johnson said: "Advertisements are…very negligently perused…" Ad readers and viewers—unless it's for something they have already bought—won't give ads close attention. There are just too many things that people would rather do. So don't puzzle them. Write copy so down-to-earth that they will read and understand it before they decide whether or not to read it.

5. Give Specific Information About Your Product/Service

When you see an ad that tells you nothing about what's being offered, you can be sure that the advertisers are throwing their money away. If you think this is rare, consider the TV commercials for automobiles—pointless special effects, 100 percent; information about the car, zero.

6. Be Brief but Readable

If you work at it, you can shave wordiness out of your message. This is important, but never make your ad hard to understand because necessary connective words have been chopped out.

7. Start with a Hook

Your first line should intrigue the viewer into reading the rest of the ad. That's the chief function of the first sentence, and it's usually the most important sentence in the ad, so sweat over it.

8. Put a Lift in the Center

If you've written a long ad, one that's two hundred words or more, you can lose readers halfway through. Put something like another hook in the middle, an offer or a bit of information that's bound to interest most of your prospective readers, to keep them reading.

9. End with a Call to Action

Be creative here. Avoid the deadly *"buy now!"* kind of weak-willed admonition that causes absolutely no one to buy now.

CHAPTER 12

Person-to-Person Selling: The Action that Gets Results

You probably won't go door to door to sell your product or service, but no matter what your occupation, you will probably benefit from understanding how to sell.

Cold Calling

Here's how to take the fear out of cold calling. Set a time to make the calls, a time when you expect to find your target people in their offices. Decide in advance how many calls you will make. Then make them fast, without pause between calls. Decide in advance that you will get turned down at least ten times before you get even a lukewarm response.

Before you begin, write out the objections you're likely to get and your answers. As you encounter new objections, jot them down, too.

Practice your cold calling technique with just you, a tape recorder, and a mirror. Why a mirror? Because if you look grim, some of your grimness will travel across the wire and affect the person you've called. Practice talking with a smile.

Use the tape recorder to play back your pitch. Work on it until you've eliminated all the uh's, ah's, and choking sounds.

Set a reasonable goal for your cold call. Many things are difficult to sell over the phone lines. In this case, the purpose of your call is to arrange a meeting with the prospect.

Painstaking Preparation Creates Powerful Presentations

Being flexible is essential because one size does NOT fit all. There are four basic types of buyers of anything. You can recognize the type you're working with at any given time, and modify your basic presentation to boost your chances of making the sale or getting the appointment with each type of person. Not only will you make more sales applying this knowledge, you'll also save time and disappointment by knowing sooner when to pack it in because you aren't going to make a particular sale.

Type 1 Buyers: The Time-Pressed

We're all pressed for time, but most of us are pretty casual about it compared to these folks. They take time seriously, and you better do the same around them. They're usually polite, but they don't waste time.

How to Sell to the "Time-Pressed"

Tell them only what they really have to know to make the decision. Avoid chitchat; it's poison with these people. Be organized and concise. And as soon as you've presented the bare bones of your case, stop chatting and ask for the order. You'll often get it.

Type 2 Buyers: The Tough Talkers

As the name implies, these people are blunt and often challenging in their comments. Often, they'll waste no time in letting you know two things: (a) they're smarter than you are, and (b) they know more about your subject than you do. Generally, they're wrong on both counts, but it's not to your advantage to try to make them admit it. They'll throw you out rather than do so. But they're barkers, not biters.

How to Sell to the "Tough Talkers"

The natural reaction is to try to convince them that in your field, you're the smooth professional and they're the bumbling amateur. You can succeed in doing so only at the cost of losing the sale. Go beyond recognizing their knowledge. Praise it so extravagantly that they start to demur a little. Then you can make your points and close the sale.

Type 3 Buyers: Friendly to a Fault

What's the most important thing to these people? They want you to like them. They want this—badly—even though your association with them will be brief. That doesn't matter to them; you are a fellow human being, and they instinctively yearn for you to show them that you like them. You might think that they're the easiest ones to sell to, and often they are, but they're impossible to sell to until they feel certain that you genuinely like them.

How to Sell to the "Friendly-to-a-Fault" Buyers

Get them talking about themselves (this won't be hard). Ask intelligent questions, pay close attention to their answers, and be fascinated by them.

Type 4 Buyers: The Reassurance Cravers

At first glance, you might think that the reassurance cravers are the same as the friendly-to-a-fault folks. Actually, they are very different. The reassurance cravers don't much care whether you like them or not; all they want is to be convinced that they're making the right move in buying from you.

How to Sell to the "Reassurance Cravers"

Stuff them full of assurances, provable claims, and guarantees—and then reassure them some more. Try this on Type 1 people and you'll be out on the street before you can say, "I should have listened to Jan Cooper." But the Reassurance Cravers can't get enough reassurance.

CHAPTER 13
Some Truths about Closing

C reative people often make mistakes that keep them from closing a sale. When they are selling their own creations, it's difficult for them not to take possible buyer comments personally. If you have a severe problem in this area, you may be well advised to sell only through galleries and other third parties.

Slick pressure tactics often result in cancellations. As you develop your sales methods, keep in mind that the only sale worth making is one that stays sold.

A lot of books have been written on the subject of closing. If you want to improve your selling percentages, read them all.

Proverbs 10:20,21
"The tongue of the just is as choice silver...
The lips of the righteous feed many."

Part Three

Your Plans and Goals Are the Rockets Powering Your Swift Soar to Success

Isa.48:17
"I am the Lord thy God
which teacheth thee to profit."

CHAPTER 14
The Success Equation

How can you improve? You do it one small step at a time. Never stop working on self-development.

I look at life as if it were a game. If you don't know the rules, you go to those who are doing what you want to accomplish and ask. How does one learn faster? By asking questions and applying what you have learned with your own experiences. From this, I have developed my own Success Equation. If you install this equation to your life and use it daily, I'm convinced that it will shorten your trial-and-error period.

Here's the Equation again:

$$TCFWY = HW + T + N + M + AQ + S + H + 7S \times PPP^2 \times P^{10}$$

Give me a moment to explain, and you'll see how really easy it is to understand it. I've simplified this equation to the point where anyone can use it to gain a happily creative life. Everyone is responsible for his or her actions. Those who need something to follow have an equation to observe and hopefully improve on.

You not only are the star of your life, you are your own director, producer, casting director, costume designer, architect, engineer, and doctor. Life is too short not to be doing what you love while you are alive. Life is too precious of a gift for that. Utilize your skills, develop your talents, prepare for a better, more peaceful you. Prepare for a better, more peaceful world.

I'm certain that my success equation will shorten your trial-and-error period, if you apply and follow it. I don't want you to think that I am a know-it-all, for all successful people have developed their own formulas, secrets, and equations, just as you will.

$$\textbf{TCFWY} = \textbf{HW} + \textbf{T} + \textbf{N} + \textbf{M} + \textbf{AQ} + \textbf{S} + \textbf{H} + \textbf{7S} \times \textbf{PPP}^2 \times \textbf{P}^{10}$$

It's not as complex as it looks when you break it down into steps, so let's look at one term at a time.

TCFWY is: *The Creative Force Within You.*
My conquering force was to create literature and products that would benefit people's lives. Writing *Argument with an Angel* was my main conquering force, and core desire. I am a problem solver. I help people solve their problems through the creations I develop. Now, what is your conquering force?

Add **HW**, it stands for *Hard Work.*
Commit yourself to working at something and overcoming obstacles until you receive what you want, even if it takes many years. It took me twenty years to write Argument with an Angel, nineteen years to find a publisher, and seventeen years to find the famous people to endorse the book. Fortunately, I was able to keep more than one of those tasks moving ahead during the same years.

Add **T**, it stands for: *Time.*
It's the clock going tick-tock, tick-tock. It's the *time* we are blessed with: seconds, minutes, hours, days, weeks, months, years, and decades spilling over into centuries. We are all blessed with *time.* The majority of people misuse time by saying, "I don't have the time." Time is all you have—use it wisely. If you want something bad enough, you will make the time to get it. You will get up two hours earlier and go to bed two hours later, for years, if you have to. When one uses his time wisely, and makes his dream a reality, it is a diamond. The years, months, days, hours, minutes, and seconds you can just think of as semiprecious and precious stones along your journey.

Add an **N**, it stands for: our *Needs*.

These are the *needs* that all of us have. By understanding our own *needs*, and helping other people with their own *needs*, we will learn how to negotiate and network to help society advance and fill the needs of a safer, more peaceful world.

Add an **M**, and it fills my mind with several powerful concepts: *Masterpiece*, *Mastermind*, and *Money*.

If we use our *money* wisely, and save a portion of everything we make, one day, we will be wealthy, and our life will be a *masterpiece*, and we will have *masterminded* it with like-minded people. Make money your slave, and it will reward you with treasures worth far more than money: time with your loved ones, and time to do what you want.

Next, add **AQ**: *Ask Questions*.

If you want something, ask and you shall receive. You can't sell without asking for the sale. You must ask yourself what it is you want out of your life, business, family, hobbies, cars, money, and so on. You must ask and make plans so you can receive. When people fail to ask questions, they are not only cheating themselves out of knowledge, they are cheating the people who want to help them.

And add an **S**, it stands for: Your *Specialty* or *Skill*.

You must know what you do best. As you search to understand what you do best—not in general, but with the utmost exactness—also work at discovering your weaknesses. It's necessary to know yourself so you can get even better. I have tried to accomplish many things because I am not afraid of failing, for that is the way you learn. Always strive to be the best that you can be, and always be prepared for when opportunities come your way. I have accomplished possibly more than some people have solely because I am prepared. Whether you are an artist, a politician, an author, a salesman, an inventor, or an actor, opportunities will come your way only because you are prepared. There are no guarantees in life. Take your *specialty* or *skill* and become a master at it. I promise you this: if you do this, you will be given another skill or talent. If you master that, you will be given another. Then you will become multitalented compared to those who choose not to use their talents.

H is for: *Health*—yours and those you love.

Many of the rich and famous would gladly give all of their money away to have their *health* restored. Having your *health*, you already are a millionaire. Would you take one million dollars for all your toes? Would you take ten million for your hands and feet? Would you take twenty million for your hearing and speech? Would you take two billion dollars for your eyes? See, you are already a billionaire, so put your resources behind you.

My Success Equation is as easy as I said it is, right? Okay, now we've gone all the way to 7S, and it was as easy as I said it would be, wasn't it?

$$\textbf{TCFWY} = \textbf{HW} + \textbf{T} + \textbf{N} + \textbf{M} + \textbf{AQ} + \textbf{S} + \textbf{H} + \textbf{7S} \times \textbf{PPP}^2 \times \textbf{P}^{10}$$

And **7S** stands for my *Seven Secrets*, which are listed below.

1. Visualize

Visualizing is picturing in your mind what it is you want to accomplish. Ever since I read the play "Everyman" at about age seventeen, I knew I wanted to write something that would benefit society and humanity. *Argument with an Angel* was a twenty-year dream, and now it's a reality. I wanted to write something that could motivate, inspire, and hopefully encourage people to put their dreams into action. I have made my dream a reality. It is your turn now to picture in your mind what it is you want to accomplish. Visualizing is planting your own seed. You know if you plant an apple seed, and the rains come, one day, you will have an apple tree. An apple tree produces hundreds and thousands of apples. This all happened from the planting of one seed. Now picture this: take one apple and try to count the seeds in one apple, much less the hundreds and thousands of apples there are. One tree, one apple, one seed can make a difference. Please visualize and plant your seed wisely.

2. Goal

This is the decision one makes as to whether or not the visualization actually takes place. How committed are you? If you give up, your visualization will not take place. You must want it so bad that you will do any ethical thing to make it happen. Every obstacle you encounter in the journey makes you stronger and wiser. The energy you put out will one day come back to honor or haunt you. So be very careful what you hope for, and what you do to arrive at your destination.

3. Plan

The majority of people are like a ship without a rudder. They put up their sails to cross the seas, to discover new lands and riches, but end up thrown against the rocks by the high winds. They sink to the bottom with their dreams still inside. Why, why, why? It is because they have failed to plan and write it down. If you don't write it down, you are not committed. If you don't have a personal and a business plan written down, you are just throwing your life to the winds of chance. Answer me this: Why would any smart person throw his life to chance?

The plan must start with a mission statement, so you know precisely what it is you want to accomplish. Write the plan down as specifically as you know how. Some of the things you write down won't happen, but offshoots come along because it was written down and you were prepared.

For instance, my whole goal, or core desire, was to write something that would benefit society. The result was my book, *Argument with an Angel*. Because I was prepared, and continually worked on self-development, all of my core desires became realities. I not only wrote *Argument with an Angel*, I also wrote *The Artists' Renaissance Course*. I ended up with six degrees, my own television show, and as a ventriloquist on a kids' television show. I have developed two workshops, *The Success Equation for Creative People* and *Goldstein's Message*, to help people reach their full potential. I have been honored with numerous awards, including the George Washington Honor Medal from the Freedom Foundation at Valley Forge. I have given the following keynote speeches:

♥ A Gift From Heaven
♥ Are You and Your Business a Rough Sketch or a Superbly Crafted Masterpiece?
♥ How to Escape Even When You're Tied Up
♥ I have a Dream: Steps to a Better, More Peaceful World
♥ I Married my Best Friend
♥ Turn Your Life into a Masterpiece

Please don't take me wrong. All these things happened because I had a plan. No matter how idealistic you are, or how lofty your goals are—your plan to save the elephants or the environment doesn't stand a chance of succeeding without a plan of action supported by your boundless enthusiasm. You have to love what you do. Write your plan down. Then start revising it as you see the need and gather more information. You are creating your own road map, your own treasure map.

4. Burning Desire

A burning desire is where you are so focused and intent on what it is you want to accomplish, that you turn your dream into an obsession. It is almost all you can think and talk about until your goal is realized. Then you develop that same drive on a new ideal or goal.

5. Faith

When things tend to go wrong, you have got to remember to keep the faith. Faith in God, faith in His Son, faith in yourself, faith in your talents, faith that you will always do what is right when temptation enters the picture. Faith that you will learn from the mistakes of the past. Faith that people will know that you are a man or woman of your word. And a continual faith in knowing that the world will become a more peaceful place.

6. **Action**

Let's look at this very important word one or two letters at a time:

A This is where you list all of your **assets**, and how they can all be used together, not just one at a time.

C Listing all your assets will give you the **courage** to move ahead.

T Use your **time** wisely and you will keep…

I **Inspiring** yourself.

O Continually inspiring yourself will put you in the **offensive** mode.

N By always being on the offensive, you will learn to control your **needs**, understand the needs of others, and learn how to negotiate and network. My mind is always in a state of action, even when I am sleeping. Do likewise. Put your dreams into action one baby step at a time.

7. **Enthusiasm**

This is the magic ingredient needed to fulfill your life's purpose. Those who love what they do are enthusiastic.

Back to the Success Equation; we're almost done with the explanations.

$$TCFWY = HW + T + N + M + AQ + S + H + 7S \times PPP^2 \times P^{10}$$

The first **P** is *Practice*. Continually *practice* to improve daily.

The second **P** is *Patience*. When things take longer than expected, wait silently and learn from the experience. Good things take a long time to develop; bad things happen fast. So learn and practice *patience*.

The third **P** is *Positioning*. You *practice patience* so you can *position* yourself to hit your target or reach your market area effectively. Move as slowly as a turtle; keep your eyes wide open like an owl's.

Notice the symbol ^{2} after **PPP**. It means you should "**square**" **PPP**, that is, multiply PPP by itself. In other words, practice patience to the max, and position yourself with the greatest possible energy.

Now multiply all the factors up to now by the final factor, **P10**, which is *Persistence to the tenth power*, which means *persistence multiplied by ten billion.*

Everything that has been mentioned so far is a waste of time if you quit or give up before you make the outcome you desire happen. If you are truly committed and persist, what you want out of life will happen. Even if it doesn't because you died in the process of making it happen, at least you lived your dream. "So, never, never, never, ever give up," as Winston Churchill said.

Let's review the Success Equation.

Begin with TCFWY by recognizing and enhancing the creative force within you.

Add **HW**, the all-important element of *Hard Work*, and add **T**, *Time*, because if you look closely at how purported "overnight successes" came about, you'll find that they were actually germinating for years.

Don't forget to add **N** for your *Needs*. While your efforts are concentrated on achieving success, you must still take care of your needs. You need exercise, recreation, family life, and to do all the other things required to live a life in balance.

If your life is out of balance, instead of sustaining you through a long drive for great accomplishments, you will break down in some way. Success will then sail out of reach. But if you do manage in your unbalanced state to grasp success, you'll find little satisfaction in it. The price your loved ones paid to get you there will turn your success into ashes.

But if you'll take care of your needs, and those of your loved ones, then to our growing list of vital elements to achieve success, let's add **M** for *Masterpiece*, *Masterminding*, and *Money*. **M** packages three essential concepts: make a *masterpiece* of your life's work, develop your skills to the *mastermind* level, and make efficient use of *money* so that you can reach your goals.

The next plus item is **AQ** for *Ask Questions*. To achieve great results, you continually need to enhance your knowledge and skills. **AQ** means not only asking other people questions, but also includes continually asking yourself what else you need to know to achieve your outcomes. When you isolate a skill or a bit of knowledge you need, do whatever it takes to acquire what you lack.

Next comes **S** for your *Specialty* or *Skill*, and **H** for enhancing your *Health.*

Plug in 7S, my *Seven Secrets*, and add seven powerful tools to aid your quest for success.

Then multiply the sum of all the foregoing elements by PPP^2. The first **P** is *Practice*. Continually *practice* to improve daily. The second **P** is *Patience*. If things take longer than expected, wait silently and learn from the experience. The third **P** is *Positioning*. You practice patience so you can *position* yourself to hit your target or reach your market area effectively.

Now we come to the final element in your new Success Equation, the formula that will guide and inspire your drive for the greatest success you can make yourself believe in. This final element is P^{10}, *Persistence to the tenth power*. Let's take a moment and think about this. It means taking what you conceive as the average amount of persistence and multiplying it by *ten billion*. I purposely chose ten billion because the number is so large that no one can really conceive of it. It's ten thousand millions. My intention is to pound home this point: your *persistence* in seeking success should vastly exceed anything you can presently imagine doing. Never stop seeking and enhancing every element of the Success Equation—and success won't be able to escape your skillful and mega-persistent pursuit.

And there you have it: a guaranteed formula for achieving your dreams.

$$TCFWY = HW + T + N + M + AQ + S + H + 7S \times PPP^2 \times P^{10}$$

When I was a young boy, I wanted to be like Superman, so I could fly as high as I wanted to go under my own power. Today, you can, too, because I have given you your cape, so you can fly high. Your cape is my Success Equation. I wanted to be like Superman so I wouldn't have to hurt so. You and your business won't have to hurt anymore, because I have given you your lead lining to protect you from Kryptonite. The lead lining is my seven secrets to creating your life's masterpiece. I wanted to be like Superman, because I loved what he represented: truth, justice, and honesty. This, I cannot give you. This, you have to earn on your own.

It's okay to be a mild-mannered Clark Kent. It's okay as long as you have built a solid foundation, and know you are Superwoman or Superman on the inside. It's okay for you to be you. It's okay to think bigger and higher thoughts, if they are within you in the first place. It's okay, so now, please take your cape and lead lining, and fly to the highest mountains to make your dreams a reality. This is an equation for success, personal and otherwise. Trust me when I say that this is not a formula to be had for the moment, or for a day or week. It's an equation for life. Become and do whatever it is you want. I'm rooting for you. What is unique about my equation? I've given you your cape so you can fly like Superman. I've given you your lead lining to protect you from Kryptonite, so you won't hurt so much. Your cape is my Success Equation. Your lead lining my seven secrets.

I'm a problem solver. How do I help people solve their problems? I take circumstances and reduce them down to their lowest common denominator. Problems come from faulty thinking on the part of people who are not using their full creativity. I just aid them as an artist in creating what it is they want solved.

If that seems too simple, consider this next fact. Simple things produce results; complex things suffer from Murphy's Law. Uncreative thinking makes simple things complex. Inventions that fail to find buyers, often, are merely more complicated ways to do something that's already being done in a simple way. Turn that around, find a simple way to do something complicated, and your fortune is made.

For example, most people don't even know what color they are personality-wise, not racially. What do I mean and how does this help? Every person is predominantly a red, yellow, blue, or green personality. By understanding the different personality types, you'll be able to close more sales. For example, if a red personality is trying to sell something to a green personality, it probably won't result in a sale.

But by understanding how a green personality responds to your question, a red personality can sell by rephrasing the question. It took me thirty years to figure out that art mirrors life.

Let's get into specifics. Let me ask you some questions so you'll see how I work. Do you consider yourself creative? Do you know how to draw? Are you ready to untie yourself and reach your full potential? Do you have problems or obstacles in your personal or business life and are looking for solutions? Fortunately for you, you are in the right place and I will share how art and creativity relate to your lives.

Do you know what parallel lines are? These lines are much like our lives; they never meet unless we have some perspectives in common. Perspective in art is being able to draw something on a flat surface so it looks three-dimensional or realistic. In real life, it's learning to keep your life in balance so you can make your dreams and goals a reality.

In art, the horizon line is the imaginary line that separates the sky from the ground or body of water. Your horizon line is your eyes and how you see things from your vantage point. Our standards and belief systems draw us together.

The vanishing point is where all parallel lines meet. In real life, this is the point where—after 1,000 doors knocked on, and after 1,000 phone calls for dates—you remain convinced that the right business opportunity or mate is just one knock or call away. Persistence pays off in the end.

In art, all parallel lines meet at a common vanishing point. In real life, all the doors you knock on and all the phone calls you make will meet at a common point of satisfaction.

By using your imagination, by focusing on your wanted results, by changing your physiology and beliefs, you will be creating the realities you want. You are your own artist, you are your own brushes, you are your own colors. You see, you are the star of your life. You can be a hero or a villain. It's the questions you ask yourself on whether you or your business will fly like a superman or sink like the *Titanic*. It's vanity that will cause you to sink.

Artists set up their own environments, just as nonartistic businesspeople do. Artists set up their easels, prepare their canvas, mix their paint, choose the appropriate brush, dim or brighten the lights, and, most important of all, prepare their state of mind. They focus on their outcome, and believe that they will turn their works of art into masterpieces. You, too, are your own artist. You have a special way of arranging your phone and your computer. You look over your appointment book, drink your coffee, and prepare your state of mind in a unique way. Focus on your need to accomplish, and believe that with that next phone call or knock on the door, you're going to make that million-dollar sale or contact.

The artist then reviews the five steps of perspective. This is where you review your mission statement, your values, your goals, the obstacles you've encountered, and how you are going to create solutions. The artist then sketches his ideas on paper or canvas; this is where you write down your ideas on paper or on the computer. This is where you and the artist are preparing for your long-term and short-term plans. Next, you and the artist become one and add detail, and become very specific on how to achieve your masterpiece. The colors an artist uses in his or her paintings bring out certain moods or emotional states of mind. The colors you wear or surround yourself with in your office or home bring about these emotional states of mind. By being creative, the artist captures our awe with his own uniqueness. Just imagine, you can be more creative and use your uniqueness to create special effects, as the artist does, for your benefit.

Okay, okay, but why do individuals and companies need more creativity? I answer best with questions because it makes you think. How many of you have had problems in your personal or business life and, if you were more creative, could have solved them quicker? How much is that worth? Hundreds, thousands, tens of thousands, and in some cases, millions of dollars? So how much do you spend on a lack of creativity?

CHAPTER 15

Make the Creative Entrepreneur's Business Plan Yours

Planning is the creative entrepreneur's second-most profitable activity. Putting the plan into action is your most profitable activity. Opening your creative gold mine sets you on the road to achieving all your goals.

Whose Journey Are You On, Yours or Someone Else's?

It's an important, fundamental question. Fortunately, in this age, when we all depend on huge corporations for many things, millions of people are content to devote their lives to making those corporations successful. I don't knock their decision; on the contrary, I applaud it. Better them than me. We can't all be entrepreneur-artists, or who would keep the phones working, fill the potholes in the highway, grow and deliver our food, and manufacture all the gadgets that make our lives more efficient and comfortable?

If you're one of the worker bees but want to strike out on your own, prepare carefully. It's not a bed of rose petals—nobody tore the thorns off so you'd be comfortable. That's your job.

When you start this journey, follow the old traveler's rule:

Take twice as much money and haul as much baggage as you can comfortably carry. On second thought, that won't be good enough; not even close. Take enough money to live on for at least six months, and get rid of all the emotional baggage you possibly can.

If You Can't Condition Yourself, Learn Other Ways to Help Yourself

You can do this by following these steps:
1. **List your faults and weaknesses.**
2. **List your strengths.**
3. **List ways to improve.**
   A. Be more open to listening and learning
   B. Study your past
   C. Apply negatives in positive ways
   D. Learn from other people's experiences
4. **Do you feel people accept you for who and what you are?** (Friends, parents, your mate)
5. **Are you yourself, or do you play games?**
      Listen to your own voice. It knows better than the others who you are. God, I thought you loved everyone. If you love us so much, how come life is so hard? Examples of the harshness of life are: Parents' divorce, your divorce, major move, death of somebody close to you, illness, business failure, and so on.

What Are Your Hold-Ups?

To find out what your hold-ups are, ask yourself the following questions:
1. How have you been conditioned since your birth?
2. Do some of your patterns need changing?
3. Do you have barriers from the past? List them by age.
   10 and under _____
   10–15 _____
   15–20 _____
   20–30 _____
   30–50 _____
   50–70 _____
   70 and higher _____

Everyone Has a Mission

To find out your mission in life, ask yourself the following questions:
1. Where do your talents lie?
2. What are you worst at?
3. How do you see yourself?
4. When do you feel your best?
5. Do you think you have a special mission?

You have probably lived through experiences that have given you special insights into certain aspects of life. Perhaps your mission is to pass that knowledge and experience on to others.

"That is a good wish for the man, sir, for to be what we are and to become what we are capable of becoming is the only aim in life."

List Your Findings

1. In just a few words (half a dozen at most), list the five most important concepts you have learned so far.
   A.
   B.
2. How are you going to apply these concepts to your life?
3. Do you believe in angels?
4. If one creates both their angels and their devils, how do you change your devils to benefit yourself and others? A wise person is not afraid to break the barriers of the past. Only by admitting faults can we overcome them and begin to grow.
5. Do you give your loved ones the time they need and deserve?
       When you find you are in error, it's best to admit to it quickly and gracefully. Those who refuse to admit error are often found out and made to look the fool.
       How do you handle a situation when you think you can't do something?
       It's good to offer a helping hand to those in need, but true help comes when you teach others the strength of their own

hands. Offering my hand should be my first act. Teaching them the freedom of their own power should be my second. This applies to countries as well as individuals.

Are you holding someone back by aiding him?

6. How do you overcome boredom and monotony?

All people suffer loneliness. Your emptiness cannot be filled by taking from others, but only by giving of oneself.

Send Yourself into A-C-T-I-O-N

A. List your Assets.

C. List the ways you are Courageous.

T. List how you will use your Time wisely.

I. Initiate productive new plans.

O. Go on the Offensive to achieve your goals.

N. Understand your Needs and the Needs of others.

Today is the only day we know we have. To live your dream, start right now. Make new friends. Start right now.

And it would be enough if it were your path. Are you a river or a lake? A river must flow through its natural course—it must move, go places, and see new things. A lake just sits there. A river can't spend its days pretending it's a lake and still be a river. If you're a river sort of person, you can't spend your days pretending you're a lake person. You must move, seek new challenges, grow, learn, and find your destiny. You are you. Only you know you.

Release Your Creative Spirit

In every work of genius, we recognize our own rejected thoughts. Emerson was so right when he said these words: "I hope through my research I can lift you up so you will take your own rejected thoughts and turn them into fine pieces of art, literature, inventions, music, and things of beauty."

A renaissance is in the making and artists and craftspeople are preparing for our rebirth. Eventually, businesspeople and laypeople will become involved when they find out how to release their creativity. By doing so, they will become happier. The engineering process has been laid. So how does one begin this process?

First, there must be preparation, where masterminding with like-minded individuals is essential. This is where the imagination soars. This is where the unexpected things arise that present us with new ideas and solutions.

Anything creative started with an idea. Then came preparation followed by execution and frustration. After twenty years or more of setbacks or 10,000 tries, whammo—Success. **Success! SUCCESS!**

Never forget that persistence is your greatest ally.

Creative people are indeed risk takers who trust their intuitions and unconscious minds. But nothing becomes a reality without action. That means pure hard work. So you better love what you are doing or get out. True creativity is finding an unusual or different way of showing others how to look at the world. Connecting your thoughts with your feelings and how they affect your body is what releases the creativity of genius. My friend, Maxine McIntyre, called it the **geni-in-us.**

True creativity only happens when people love what they do and commit their life's work to that endeavor. Persistence, as Edison said, is the genius. The one who makes the most mistakes is the creative person—the one who is not willing to give up. Sometimes, people are like old paint. At times, when paint is old, it becomes transparent and you can see the original lines underneath. When a person accomplishes something and it becomes a reality, then you can go back and see his or her original steps underneath that made it a reality.

Creativity comes when one has been prepared and committed himself or herself into action. We create our own lives of happiness or of desperation.

Seven Secrets to Creating Your Life's Masterpiece

Most people leave out one of the seven secrets to creating your life's masterpiece—faith—and it prevents them from succeeding. I believe that anyone who lacks faith cannot be truly creative. Without purpose, one cannot have faith. Creative people usually have to find assistance before they can turn their ideas into realities. Ford, Disney, and Bill Gates did.

I've been an art teacher for most of my life. Someday, we will have teachers willing to stretch themselves to become the most they are capable of. This will inspire our students to do the same thing. To attract teachers who are creative and know how to bring out our youths' full potential, we have to be compensated in a different manner than today. The teacher of tomorrow will be multitalented; mediocrity will not even be considered.

As a society, we must learn to teach not only how to learn, but how to accomplish and persevere with what has been learned. A true leader or teacher helps people to stretch themselves to go further than they could have on their own.

However, creativity does have its dark side. You must know yourself and on which side you stand. Yes, we do have Ghandis and Mother Theresas, but we also have Hitlers. Are you searching for creative ways to be famous or infamous? Only you know your true trails, like Roy Rogers's "Happy Trails."

True creativity comes from the artist, author, sculptor, inventor, musician—the person who is not afraid to take risks. Then others—the politician, the teacher, the businessperson—come aboard and take the credit. America will always be the most creative place on the face of this earth for one reason, and only one reason. The reason being that people from all walks of life and countries from all over the world are striving and struggling to come to a land where there is opportunity.

I love what Thoreau wrote: "If one advances in the direction of his dreams, one will meet with success unexpected in common hours." An American renaissance is in the making, and in due time, a world renaissance will be appearing. The famous and the infamous will appear upon playing grounds similar to a checkerboard. Good against bad, peace against violence, truth against evil.

Which side will you stand on?

Everything depends upon our actions. A world of peace or of devastation—blame no one but yourself if your world crumbles. Jim

Rohn said, "Unless you change what you are, you will always have what you've got."

Jim also stated another important concept in words similar to these.

You are what you are because of the choices you've made in the past. You must become a reader if you want to become a leader. Put words into your mind that will resemble the colors of an artist's palette. By reading you will learn how to persuade and convince. These are your seeds to getting what you want. If you want something bad enough, you will find a way to make it happen. When you take this knowledge and learn, search, and apply, your miracles will begin to happen.

By Helping Others, You Help Yourself

Remember where you have come from and how you got to where you are. Every now and then, I go back to my old neighborhood just to remind myself of where I have come from. Help others to understand that they are where they are now because of the choices they have made in the past. Never attack a person, but always attack the problem and help them to solve it. Help people to see themselves as they are, and show them solutions based on what they can become.

Make a pledge to yourself to help as many people as you can during the twenty-first century through your products and services. You will have to become multitalented just to survive. So you must use all of your talents. Zig Zigler said two things that have stuck in my mind over the years. They are: "If you help enough people to get what they want, you will get what you want." And, "Money isn't everything, but it ranks right up there with oxygen."

Jim Rohn said, "Success is something you attract by the person you become. So get rid of your needs and start planting seeds." You must plant seeds to reap a harvest. He also stated, "Failure is a few errors in judgment made every day, and success is a few simple easy disciplines done every day." I gather from this that no matter how wise you are, if your wisdom is not invested and used, it is wasted.

How You Can Make a Difference

Thoreau said, "Things do not change, we change." When their lives get too bad, some people commit suicide. Others reject this ultimate admission of failure, reform themselves, and become what they wanted to be in the first place.

What is it that you want for yourself? Here are four ways you can make a difference:

1. **Service to Your Community**
   Decide right now how you are going to serve mankind. Then find someone you can help and someone who can help you.

2. **Spirit of Service**
   Love is spirit; ego is fear. Are you speaking from love or fear? Risk more than others are willing to do. Expect more than others believe is possible. Dream more than others think is practicable.

3. **Spreading Your Spiritual Light and Service**
   Edith Wharton said, "There are two ways of spreading light: To be the candle, or the mirror that reflects it." To me, this means that you create or duplicate yourself.

4. **Make a Difference Globally**
   Be thankful for this moment. Whoever shows up in your life is meant to be. They are your angels for the moment. Learn from this moment, for it is soon gone.

How to Excel at Controlling Your Needs

The first thing you must do is to identify the areas that need working on. The overcoming in these areas helps you to motivate yourself and help others. Now, ask yourself these questions:

1. How is my future going to be on the path I'm on?
2. How could my future be if I choose to change?
3. Who exactly am I?
4. What is my greatest accomplishment?
5. What am I doing now that I'm not proud of?
6. What are my personal strengths?
7. In what areas do I need to improve?
8. What is my major goal in life?
9. What would I do if I had one year to live? One month? One week? One day? One hour? One minute? One second?

Proverbs 27:20
"The eyes of man are never satisfied."

CHAPTER 16

The Plan and Your Goals

The Secrets of Communicating with Yourself so You Can Communicate with Others

E xplain who you are in one to three sentences.
Let's assume that a statue is being built in your honor because of your accomplishments. What would you want on the plaque? What motivates you? How do you deal with conflict? Be specific. It will help you to reach your goals sooner.

Jim Rohn said:
Conflict only occurs when we want two things at the same time and have the desire to do them both. One way leads to *success* the other to *failure*—it's your choice. The greatest political and spiritual leaders share a common thread—they are great storytellers. From their vast inventory of stories they can always pull one for every point they want to make. Try to tell only your own stories, but if you tell someone else's story, give them credit. Success is the steady progress of making your goals a reality.

He's right, but to me, it's the steady progress of using your time wisely to make your dream a reality. Take your time and tell your stories, and develop them. Either way, you will pay a price.
You'll pay the price of regret, where you will suffer the pain, or the price of discipline, where you will achieve your rewards. Although there's no gain without pain when you strive for greater things,

stagnation is not a way in which you can escape pain. The most persistent pain of all is the pain of regret.

I'm paraphrasing Jim Rohn again. He said something like this: The difference between the rich and the poor is the rich invest their money first and spend what is left. The poor spend all of their money and invest what is left.

Work with the people who deserve it, not those who need it. You must reap before you sow, so plant your seeds and count the apples in each seed. John Stuart Mill said, "It is better to be Socrates dissatisfied, than a pig satisfied."

What Are Your Viewpoints?

Success is nothing more than achieving what it is you want for your life and being able to look in the mirror at the end of your life. Quit listening to others! People self-destruct because they listen to the negative comments of those around them about their dreams. Eric Butterworth said, "Nothing stops the man who desires to achieve." Dreams keep one going; goals and plans keep one on course.

So what are your viewpoints? How do you see yourself? Do you tend to see things in a negative way or do you lean to the positive?

Thomas Jefferson said, "Opportunity—missed by most people because it is dressed in overalls and looks like work." Fifty percent of the people are beat if you just decide to work hard and show up. Forty percent of the rest are beat if you are honest and say and do what you say you will. That is ninety percent of the people.

The last ten percent must see further, listen closer, speak less, and give to the public through products and services what they need and what they want.

So it is your viewpoints that will decide where you will be at the end of your life.

Dare to Dream

Zig Zigler said, "Dream as far as you can go; and when you get there you can see further." You have dreams. Everyone has dreams.

Unfortunately, most people give up on theirs. But you won't be the one to give up on your dreams, will you? Let's look at some people who did not give up on their dreams.

Years ago, children used to die from contaminated milk. A drifter dreamed of helping the children. Because of this dream, Borden's Milk and Ice Cream was founded by Gail Borden.

Two friends set up shop in their garage, dreaming of setting new trends in technology. If not for them, we wouldn't have Hewlett-Packard, founded by William Hewlett and David Packard.

Another two friends, Steve Jobs and Steve Wozniak, created the first Apple computer in their garage and launched a company that would leap into the ranks of the Fortune 500 with amazing speed.

Two brothers tinkering in their bicycle shop invented the wind tunnel to test their theories—and made the first ever flight in a heavier-than-air vehicle.

One individual dreamed of escaping from the mines in his home state of Pennsylvania. Being a good athlete, he followed his dream, and ended up a pro-football player and coach of the Chicago Bears, Mike Ditka.

Two brothers dreamed of serving one product in thirty-one different ways, and from their efforts, we now have Baskin-Robbins, founded by Burton Baskin and Irvine Robbins.

A teenager grew up very lonely and dreamed of becoming a radio announcer with his own show. From that dream came American Bandstand, founded by Dick Clark.

Accomplishing your dream is the greatest reward and feeling one can experience, so never consider your worst thoughts and quit. When you become frustrated, you must quadruple the effort and reward yourself along the way. When you learn how to take the complicated and reduce it into simple form, then you will be called a genius.

The real power of not having a job but having an Internet business is that you have a chance to live your life—live the lifestyle you want, and not be tied down to a paycheck or the daily grind. You've got loads of money. You can go on vacation when you want, do what you want, and basically live your life in a fashion that's agreeable to you. Read the following testimonies from real people in today's world.

Dr. Jan Cooper

Fat Little Kid to Renaissance Man in Forty Years

When I was a young boy, I was told that I had a speech impediment. I used to reverse letters, words, and numbers around, and occasionally still do. Today, as a mature man, I am said to be an author, speaker, artist, and teacher. I, perhaps, could be so humble, or maybe I have been humbled by life, that I could admit to the correctness of that assessment of my young life. I now realize that I am still just that schoolboy. But here is how I got from that fat little kid, who was labeled as a slow learner, to a seventy-year-old author, speaker, artist, and teacher.

Through my own stumbling and learning, I have developed my own personal Success Equation for life. Every year, from now on, I am going to give away two American Renaissance Awards. I will award one to the person who overcomes the most in his or her personal life, and one who takes his or her talents and accomplishes the most with them.

If you knew you could do anything—and knew you could not fail—what would you attempt? Clement Stone and Napoleon Hill said in words like these: "If you can conceive of an idea, and believe it, you can achieve it." I, too, believe this from my trial-and-error methods, and am able to fill in some steps to hopefully make your life a little easier and shorten your learning path. So, will you please learn from other people's experiences, as my friend and mentor, Cavett Robert, would say?

Wherever you are, at this point in your life, first find out what it is you want to do. For, you see, it is your life, and nobody can live it for you. You are your own artist. You are your own brushes. You are your own colors. You see, you are the star of your life. You can be a hero, a villain, or just lead a plain, mediocre life in quiet desperation, as Emerson would say. It is your choices and attitudes that will make or break you. But there are four things that you can do so you won't be in the same position five, ten, fifteen, twenty-five, or thirty years from now:

1. The kind of books you read;
2. The kind of CD'S you listen to and the DVD'S you watch;

3. The kind of workshops and seminars you attend; and
4. Most important of all, the kind of people you choose to associate with.

CHAPTER 17

Harness the Power of Effective Goal Setting

The concept behind effective goal setting is straightforward. Here are the points you need to cover:

1. **Decide** exactly what you want to achieve. In other words, define what your goal #1 will be.
2. **List** all of the things you must do to achieve #1.
3. **List** all of the things you spend time, money, and energy on that don't contribute directly to #1.
4. **Decide** which items on List 3 that you'll stop doing to release time, money, and energy for #1.
5. **Go back over** 3 and 4, and this time, get realistic. If you really want #1, how much of your resources are you going to piddle away on these time-wasters?
6. **Now create** a plan for achieving #1.
7. **Reexamine** steps 1 through 6 and resolve any conflicts in favor of accomplishing #1.
8. **Now analyze** #1.

   Is it something you passionately want? Is it something you'll have to push yourself to achieve? Is it something you wholeheartedly believe you can achieve? Unless you can answer yes to all three questions, you need to reconsider #1. It may be so high that you don't believe in it; it may be so low that it doesn't excite you. Make sure that #1 is a believable challenge that excites you.

   After you have set goal #1 and are making steady progress toward it, you may want to set additional, nonconflicting goals in different areas of your life.

The Basis of It All: The Efficient Schedule

Lots of organizers, both paper and electronic, can be found in office supply stores. The marvelous PalmPilot is indispensable to many busy people. Entries can be made anywhere on it. You can even transfer data to and from a desktop computer.

Keeping an organizer of some kind handy throughout your workday is the first step toward operating on an efficient schedule.

Efficient Budgeting and Financial Control in the Computer Age

Programs such as Intuit's Quicken or QuickBooks® turn any desktop computer into a machine capable of handling budgeting, check writing, taxes, and complete financial control of a business and investment portfolio, and more.

Many of the largest news-gathering organizations in the world will e-mail news about the subjects you're interested in to you—and they'll do it for free! Online connections also permit rapid purchasing of everything you formerly had to drive somewhere to buy, thus saving you large amounts of time.

Power, Success, and Fortune for Personal and Business Pleasure

Throughout history, people have wanted POWER, trying to be number one; the top of the heap. Many people today can have this ingredient if they take their knowledge and put it into action. But the difficult part is figuring out how to take a person's dreams and turn them into a reality. So one must know why he wants something; he must recognize his weaknesses and strengths. He must know what he can really do and what results he expects and the effort he is willing to put forth. He must know himself to have POWER.

By failing, we learn. It is our failures that make us and take us to our highest potentials. By learning from our failures and combining that with ACTION, we are on our way to success. The true secret, formula, or equation, to success, whether you be a businessman, an artist, an author, or a scientist, is that each of us have a sense of purpose and live our dreams. The people who live their dreams have a productive and happy life. They also work on themselves daily, continually striving for improvement in every aspect of their lives. These habits are powerful tools that were developed one baby step at a time.

In my youth, I was blessed with negative thinking, inferiority complex, being labeled a slow learner, placed in remedial classes, and, yes, even reversing my words, letters, and numbers around. I was blessed because I learned how to eliminate bad habits and replace them with positive ones. I'm not perfect. I still have areas in my life that I'm working on, just as we all will till the day we leave this wonderful world. The greatest secret, if there is a secret, is using your time wisely and striving to overcome in all areas of your life.

Sir Laurence Olivier said in words similar to these: "USE YOUR WEAKNESSES; ASPIRE TO STRENGTH."

You say you want POWER, SUCCESS, and FORTUNE, then this is what you must do. You must find out what it is that most people want and find a way to help them get it. You must help them solve their problems by making their lives easier, simpler, and happier.

CHAPTER 18
Juicy Morsels

Secrets of Leadership
By Napoleon Hill

Unwavering courage, self-control, a keen sense of justice, definiteness of purpose and plans, the habit of doing more than paid for, a pleasing personality, sympathy and understanding, mastery of detail, willingness to accept full responsibility, and cooperation. The world pays you for what you do or can induce others to do. Concentrate on what you can give.

The greatest tragedy of life consists of men and women who earnestly try and fail.

There Are Thirty Reasons for Failure:

1. Unfavorable Hereditary Background
2. Lack of a Well-Defined Purpose
3. Lack of Ambition to Rise Above Mediocrity
4. Insufficient Education
5. Lack of Self-Discipline: If you do not conquer self, you will be conquered by self. Self-mastery is the hardest job you will ever have. By stepping in front of the mirror, you will see that you are your best friend and your worst enemy.
6. Ill Health
7. Unfavorable Environmental Influences During Childhood
8. Procrastination
9. Lack of Persistence
10. Negative Personality

11. Lack of Controlled Sexual Urges

12. Uncontrolled Desire to Have Something for Nothing

13. Lack of a Well-Defined Power of Decision

14. Have One or More of the Six Basic Fears: Poverty, Criticism, Ill Health, Old Age, Death, and Lost Love

15. Wrong Selection of a Mate in Marriage

16. Overcautious

17. Wrong Selection of Business Associates

18. Superstition and Prejudice

19. Wrong Vocation

20. Lack of Concentration

21. Overspending

22. Lack of Enthusiasm

23. Intolerance—People with Closed Minds on Religious, Racial, and Political Differences of Opinion

24. Intemperance—Overindulging in Anything

25. Inability to Cooperate with Others

26. Possession of Power that Was Not Acquired through Self-Effort

27. Intentional Dishonesty

28. Egotism and Vanity

29. Lack of Capital

30. Guessing Instead of Thinking

What Are Your Leadership Qualities?
Think and Grow Rich
By Napoleon Hill

1. All achievements, and all earned riches, have their beginning in an idea. So, let's learn how to make life say yes instead of no to your plans and ambitions. Make up your mind, whatever it is you decide you want to do, to stay until you succeed. Adopt a definite purpose. R. U. DARBY.

2. When riches begin to come, they come so quickly, in such great abundance that one wonders where they have been hiding all of those lean years. Success comes to those who become success

conscious. Henry Ford V-8 engine. The longer you work in the right direction, the closer you are to success. Dreams come true when desire transforms them into concrete action, with a plan, and persistence. Wishing will not bring riches. You must give before you receive. So, see yourself rendering service or delivering merchandise. Pages 49 and 52.

3. There are two kinds of knowledge: GENERAL and SPECIALIZED. Knowledge will not attract money, unless it is organized and intelligently directed, through practical plans of action. Knowledge is only potential power. It becomes POWER when it is organized into definite plans of action and to a definite end with enthusiasm.

4. There are two kinds of imagination: SYNTHETIC IMAGINATION—through this faculty, one arranges old concepts, ideas, and plans into new combinations. You work with your experiences, education, and observations on which it is fed. This faculty is used most by the inventor. CREATIVE IMAGINATION—a genius draws from this process. This is where hunches and inspirations are received. This is where all basic and new ideas come from. This works automatically through the emotion of a strong desire. Great leaders of business, industry, finance, poets, writers, artists, and musicians become great because they have developed the faculty of CREATIVE IMAGINATION. The story of every great fortune begins when a creator of ideas and a seller of ideas get together and work in harmony. So, surround yourself with the people who can do what you cannot. The finest tool still needs a person who knows how to use it.

CREATE A MASTERMIND GROUP. This group should meet twice a week. Only allow people in your group who can work in perfect harmony. No person can acquire a fortune without the cooperation of other people. Remember, a quitter never wins, and a winner never quits. There are two types of people: leaders and followers. Most great leaders began as followers. They became great because they were intelligent followers.

POWER, SUCCESS, AND FORTUNE FOR PERSONAL AND BUSINESS PLEASURE

Throughout history people have wanted POWER trying to be number one, top of the heap. Many people today can have this ingredient if they take their knowledge and put it into action. But the difficult part is figuring out how to take a person's dreams and turn them into a reality. One must know why they want something. They must recognize their weaknesses and strengths. You must know what you really can do and what results you expect and the effort you are willing to put forth. You must know yourself to have POWER.

By failing we learn. It is our failures that make us and take us to our highest potential. By learning from our failures and combining that with ACTION, you are on your way to success. The true secret formula, or equation to success, whether you be a businessman, artist, author, or scientist is that each of these individuals have a sense of purpose and live their dream. The people who live their dream have a productive and happy life. They also work on themselves daily and continually strive for improvement in every aspect of their life. These habits are powerful tools that were developed one baby step at a time.

In my youth, I was blessed with negative thinking, inferiority complexes, being labeled a slow learner, placed in remedial classes and yes even reversing my words, letters, and numbers around. I was blessed because I learned how to eliminate bad habits and replace them with positive habits. I'm not perfect. I still have areas in my life I'm working on just as we all will until the day we leave this wonderful world. The greatest secret if their is a secret is using your time wisely and striving to overcome in all areas of your life. Sir Laurence Olivier said in words similar to these, "USE YOUR WEAKNESSES; ASPIRE TO STRENGTH."

You say you want POWER, SUCCESS, AND FORTUNE. Then this is what you must do. You must find out what it is that most people want and find a way to help them get it. You must help them solve their problems by making their lives easier, simpler, and happier.

A Short Story

One day, an expert in time management was speaking to a group of business students. To drive home a point, he used an illustration that those students would never forget. As he stood in front of the group of high-powered overachievers, he said, "Okay, time for a quiz." Then he pulled out a one-gallon, wide-mouthed Mason jar and set it on the table in front of him. He produced about a dozen fist-sized rocks and carefully placed them one at a time into the jar. When the jar was filled to the top and no more rocks would fit inside, he asked, "Is this jar full?" Everyone in the class said yes. Then he said, "Really?" He reached under the table and pulled out a bucket of gravel. Then he dumped some gravel in and shook the jar, causing pieces of gravel to work themselves down into the space between the big rocks. Then he asked the group once more, "Is the jar full?" By this time, the class was onto him.

"Probably not," one of them answered.

"Good," he replied. He reached under the table and brought out a bucket of sand. He started dumping the sand in the jar and it went into all of the spaces left between the rocks and the gravel. Once more, he asked the question, "Is this jar full?"

"No," the class shouted.

And again, he replied, "Good." He grabbed a pitcher of water and began to pour it in until the jar was filled to the brim. Then he looked at the class and asked, "What is the point of this illustration?"

One eager person raised his hand and said, "The point is, no matter how full your schedule is, if you try really hard, you can always fit some more things in it."

"No," the speaker responded, "that's not the point."

The truth that this illustration teaches us is, if you don't put all the big rocks in first, you'll never get them in at all.

What are the big rocks in your life? Your children, your loved ones, your education, your dreams, a worthy cause, teaching or mentoring others, doing things that you love, time for yourself, your health, your significant other.

Remember to put these BIG ROCKS first or you'll never get them in at all. If you sweat all the little stuff (the gravel, the sand), then you'll fill your life with little things you worry about that don't really matter, and you'll never have the real quality time you need to spend on the big, important stuff (the big rocks).

So tonight, or in the morning, when you are reflecting on this short story, ask yourself this question: What are the "big rocks" in my life?

Put those in your jar first!

CHAPTER 19
Create, Sell, and Become Rich

D o you really want to Create, Sell, and Become Rich? Let's find out if you are serious. Do you have credit cards? Do you have habits you want to overcome? Do you have a mortgage payment? Are you paying all of your bills on time? Would you like to be financially independent? Do you really believe you can be? Are you doing anything about it now? If you had no bills, what would you do? If you didn't have to worry about money, what would you be doing this very moment? Are you ready to learn things that you can do to become financially independent?

Are you willing to do what you must so you can pay cash for everything? Are you ready to start on your path to never having to worry about money again? Are you ready to pay the price to be rich? Are you ready to sell yourself on the idea of creating a new you?

If you believe it is possible to be debt free and living a life of luxury, you can have it within five to ten years. It will be your choice to get in the habit of paying cash for everything. Napoleon Hill said, "If you can see it, and believe it, you can achieve it." Yes, if you can create the dream and sell yourself on it; you can become rich. Now let's take some simple steps to no longer being a slave and living debt free.

Albert Einstein said, "Try not to become a man of success but rather try to become a man of value." You are now in the process of eliminating debt and becoming a person of value and the director of your own life.

Another wise man, James Allen, stated, "A man sooner or later discovers that he is the master gardener of his soul, the director of his life." You are the star and director of your own life. There is a price to be paid for growing rich. Instant gratification promises gain without pain. Debt is like a drug. You are in debt because you have always wanted instant gratification. And debt, like a drug, will one day work against you. You must work smart while you are young, or you'll be working hard when you are old.

The final step on your way to riches is to cut up all your credit cards and promise yourself to never ever use them again. If you do this, you'll be saving yourself between ten to twenty percent a year. That's a good investment in itself. Once all credit cards are paid off, apply those same payments to additional principal on your mortgage. Quit smoking and apply that to the principal on your mortgage. Add up all the extras and apply those to the principal of your mortgage. Buy a one- or two-year-old car and pay cash for it, and apply the difference toward the mortgage on your home. Quit investing and apply all monies to the principal on your mortgage. It will be worth it to you.

Your goal should be to pay off all of your debts in the shortest amount of time. When your mortgage is paid, you will have saved between $200,000 and $600,000 on a thirty-year mortgage and completely paid off in five to ten years.

Now that you're debt free and have broken the chains of slavery, invest to the maximum and pay cash for everything.

Janis Joplin stated, "Don't compromise yourself. You are all you've got." Remember not to compromise yourself. Your on your way to becoming financially independent. The next ten years will fly by rapidly and you will be glad you took these steps to wealth.

Sallust said, "Every man is the architect of his own fortune." You owe it to yourself to be a master, not a slave. Change yourself and your habits, and you will grow rich.

Orison Suitt Marden stated, "Our destiny changes with our thoughts; we shall become what we wish to become, do what we wish to do, when our habitual thought corresponds with a desire." May your desires be so great that you will change your habits so you can Create, Sell, and Grow Rich. Yes, if you change yourself, you will change your world. At this moment, you are changing. You are creating ideas. You are selling yourself on the idea of eliminating debt so you can grow rich.

Napoleon Hill stated in his book, *Think and Grow Rich*, "There are no limitations to the mind except those we acknowledge. Both poverty and riches are the offspring of thought." You are where you are now because of your past thoughts. You are now on a journey of acquiring wealth. Please write and tell me of your progress.

What wise words Les Hewitt used as they flowed from his lips: "Your habits and belief systems are a product of your environment. A person brought up in a negative environment, continually subjected to physical or verbal abuse, will have a different view of the world than a child reared in a warm, loving, and supportive family." Whether you've come from an abusive environment or not, I want you to know that someone cares. I want you to know that others have overcome and you can, too. Your thoughts are so powerful that they will determine your future, so please, never ever delay your future again with a negative thought.

The billionaire J. Paul Getty said, "The individual who wants to reach the top in business must appreciate the might of the force of habit, and must understand that practices are what creates habits. He must be quick to break those habits that can break him—and hasten to adopt those practices that will become the habits that will help him achieve the success he desires."

You have my permission to quit bad habits. You know you need to. You now have permission to start your journey to wealth. You can now start by paying off your smallest bill. After it is paid off, you apply it to your next bill and keep going down the chain until all debts are paid in full. Then apply the same amount of money that was going out on your bills to the principal on your mortgage, and within five to ten years, you will be living debt free and become financially independent.

You will soon be living your dream, the life you've always wanted—just by changing a few habits. So, please, create new ideas and habits, sell yourself on the change, and in the process, let time help you to grow rich.

Master Your Life

Fellow businessperson and entrepreneur,

I want you to know that God has a plan for your life. It is a plan of good, not evil. It will give you hope and a future. You are special. You are as precious as a jewel; like a lump of coal, you have been developing your skills and talents that are now at the level of a diamond! You have DREAMS! God put those DREAMS in your mind. But they will only happen if you act upon them.

"Let your light so shine before men, that they may see your good works, and glorify your Father which is in heaven" Matthew 5:16.

Whatever your talents may be, let them be of such a high quality that all men will know that your creations were to honor and glorify our Father, which art in heaven, giving Him all the credit.

Action is the key to anything real or imagined! An American Renaissance is in the making and artists and crafts people are preparing for our rebirth! A rebirth that will unite you with what God has called you to do. Only you know what that is.

"And Saul sought to smite David even to the wall with the javelin; but he slipped away out of Saul's presence, and he smote the javelin into the wall; and David fled, and escaped the night." 1 Samuel 19:10.

You, too, must escape if you want a new you. You must invest in yourself and your future, and pay off all debts ASAP.

ALWAYS STRIVE TO EARN AS MUCH AS YOU CAN, SO YOU CAN SAVE AS MUCH AS YOU CAN, SO YOU CAN INVEST AS MUCH AS YOU CAN, SO YOU CAN GIVE AS MUCH AS YOU CAN.

Everyone has two problems that need to be solved:
1. Everyone wants an opportunity!
2. Everyone needs a mental enema!

Give people what they need: an opportunity and a mental enema.
Ralph Oats

Obstacles

(Short Story)
Contributed by Lee Ryan Miller

The Obstacle in Our Path

I n ancient times, a king had a boulder placed on a roadway. Then he hid himself and watched to see if anyone would remove the huge rock.

Some of the king's wealthiest merchants and courtiers came by and simply walked around it. Many loudly blamed the king for not keeping the roads clear, but none did anything about getting the big stone out of the way.

Then a peasant carrying a load of vegetables came along. On approaching the boulder, the peasant laid down his burden and tried to move the stone to the side of the road. After much pushing and straining, he finally succeeded. As the peasant picked up his load of vegetables, he noticed a purse lying in the road where the boulder had been. The purse contained many gold coins and a note from the king, indicating that the gold was for the person who removed the boulder from the roadway.

The peasant learned what many others never understand. Every obstacle presents an opportunity to improve one's condition.

How I Overcame My Obstacles

During the time I was visualizing my dreams becoming a reality, my wife and I were living with very little money. I remember seeing myself with a book I wrote while at the same time setting several plastic garbage cans around the house to catch the rainwater leaking through the roof. I pictured myself as a professional speaker, up in front of an appreciative audience of 100,000 while I walked door-to-door, selling WTF tear gas (now they use pepper spray and zap guns). Our car was in such bad shape that the kids would ask to be left off two blocks from the school so no one would see them getting out of a junker. Just as soon as I fixed the heater, the refrigerator broke down. It seemed like we would never get ahead.

But we kept our spirits up. We kept our faith in God. Like Job, He tested us to see if we really believed His Word, and whether we would really stay true to our beliefs. We did, and He rewarded us. He increased skills and brought out talents in me that I had not known I had.

Unless born into a wealthy family, many famous people have gone through this refining process of turning coal into diamonds. The key is to learn as you go through the hurt and pain. I believe I am called to help people who find themselves in this situation.

The Purpose of Your Life

We're all given one life here on earth, so you might as well take advantage of it. Live your dream now; you cannot do it when you are dead. Even if your dream is just a hobby, put time and energy into it. It is better to use it a little than not at all. You know that when you are doing what you want to do, you are truly happy.

On a talk show, people were asked what they wanted to be when they grew up. Most did not raise their hand; they did not know. Why is this? It is because they did not ask the right question. Some people don't want to work and pay the price for excellence, so they will never get there. You can wish to be an author, wish to be an artist, or a movie star. But only hard work is going to get you there.

Yes, hard work! Mentors, coaches, and those who have influenced your life will help you to reach your final destination. Here are a few names who have influenced my life: Wally Cato, Jack Canfield, Lou Holtz, Tom Hopkins, Ira Hayes, Cavett Robert, Dennis Waitly, Charlie Tremendous Jones, Donald Trump, John Travolta, Dennis Turner, Mark Victor Hansen, Dottie Walters, Linda Forsythe, Brian Tracy, Zig Ziggler, Art Linkletter, Arnold Schwarzennegger, and many others.

Jan Cooper

Jan Cooper, as an undergraduate, has degrees in speech, drama, and art. His advanced degrees include a master's degree in education from Oregon State University, and a PhD from the American Institute of Holistic Theology.

Jan has taught art to troubled inner-city youths and some of his students have won the American Automobile Association Award for Excellence, as well as scholarships to Walt Disney Studios and a fashion design school.

Jan has hosted his own TV show, interviewing artists and authors. For a couple of years, he was the ventriloquist on a children's TV show. He, also, is a graduate gemologist and jewelry designer from the Gemological Institute of America in Santa Monica.

His most prestigious award and honor is the George Washington Honor Medal from the Freedom Foundation at Valley Forge. He is a member of several speakers' associations, workshop associations, and a member of the American Association of Christian Counselors. He was with the Hope Wellness Institute for nearly two years, located in St. George Medical Center. After thirty-three years of teaching, Jan retired to do what he promised God he would do when he was a young man.

"When I was young, I was placed in remedial classes, told I had a speech impediment, and that my IQ was not high enough for academic work. From my experience as a student and a teacher, I believe it is very harmful to label a student. So I have created products and services that will help people reach their full potential. For you see, you are your own artist! You are your own brushes! You are your own colors! You are the star of your life! My definition of success is getting into a position where you are doing what you love and helping other people to do what they love. You get there with my Success Equation. You cannot be in it just for the money, however. The people who love what they do and are providing a service to mankind to make people's lives easier are the people who are rewarded financially."

Faith in God

Faith in God has been an underlying thread from which is woven the fabric of life. I believe that faith in God is crucial to success in life. Someone raised in another country might call it faith in their god. But they need to have a faith in a power higher than themselves. I do believe in God. I believe in Jesus. I am a Christian. But even people who don't have the same belief as a Christian need to have that same simple belief that there is a power greater than themselves. I promised God when I was young that when I became accomplished in certain areas by Him giving me the talents and skills, I would let people know where the power came from. And that's what I'm doing right now.

I talk to Jesus every day and every night. He has helped me along the whole way. When I was a fat little kid, I was placed in remedial classes where I was called dumb and stupid. Without faith in Him, I would have crumbled.

God has been intervening and taking care of me my whole life. I don't think I could have written all the books I have without Him. I don't think I could be putting together these workshops and keynote speeches. After all, I flunked English in high school and college. I know he is using me because I am creative and open to Him.

That is what convinced me that there is a God! For some reason, I have always believed in God. I don't know how or why. But deep down inside, I knew intuitively, even as a child, that I needed faith in Him. I always felt that He was there for me, talking to me, giving me that tingly feeling when I looked at stars. When no one else cared, He did.

In conclusion, I do not want you to live your life with unfulfilled dreams and desires. I want you to have all that life offers. If you knew you could do anything in the world and you knew you could not fail, what would you do? Whatever this is, do it. Follow my Success Equation and watch your dreams materialize, with God's help

When this happens, miracles do happen.

Miracles Do Happen

The choice you make may make the difference. One minute can change your whole life.

One Saturday afternoon, I was meeting a friend for lunch downtown. I am usually one-half hour early everywhere I go. Since having some free time, a pocket watch caught my attention in a jewelry store window across from the restaurant.

Upon entering the jewelry store, I saw the most beautiful person in the world. I spurted out, "I need your phone number." For some reason, she gave it to me. Our MIRACLE happened and we have been together now for forty years. My MIRACLE happened. NOW, it is time to prepare you for yours.

Your Miracle

To fully produce your DREAM and prepare for your MIRACLE you will develop a BURNING DESIRE. This is where you are so focused and intent on what it is you want to accomplish, that you turn your DREAM into an obsession. It is almost all you can think about until your goal is realized. Then you develop the same drive on a new goal or DREAM!

When things tend to go wrong, you have got to remember to learn from the past, live in the present, and plan for the future. Remember to keep your FAITH! Faith in God, faith in His Son, faith in your talents, faith that you will always do what is right when TEMPTATION enters the picture. Faith that people will know you are a man or woman of your word, and a continual faith that we will try to make this a better more peaceful world. Miracles are coming towards you or passed you every second. It is up to you to recognize them. Your weeds will become WHEAT at just the right TIME!

Pick up your Bible and repeat after me: THIS HOLY BOOK! MY FAVORITE BOOK! HAS THE HOLY SPIRIT FLOWING ALL THE WAY THROUGH IT! ALL THE WAY THROUGH IT! ENTERING INTO MY HEART! ENTERING INTO YOUR HEART! CREATING

THE DREAMS AND PLANS GOD HAS FOR EACH AND EVERY ONE OF US!

Independent Learning Contract

What did I learn?

What are some examples that will benefit your personal, business, and social life?

What other resources should I use?

Did I gain all I could from this unit?

Give some examples of possible use of the information in this unit:
1. personal life
2. business life
3. social life

How many people and of what type will help you reach your goal?

As you gain more information, you may change your goal slightly, so you will be defining your goal at the end of each unit. Restate your goal. Be specific.

Jan Cooper of North Highlands, Calif., is unique among sales trainers and motivational speakers because he invites any three people from the audience to "come on stage and tie me up with a rope." He delivers his polished and effective presentations while, Houdini-like, he "gets loose" before his audience. Cooper is a published author of three books, a TV personality, an educator and a painter whose artworks are now in more than 33 U.S. galleries coast to coast. He is highly experienced in talking to sales executives in all financial disciplines. Cooper is represented by the FSA Speaker's Bureau. Jan Cooper is often called "The Renaissance Man" and is frequently asked back by his audiences.

Footnotes

. William Mize, *Trust Marketing Execu-*͏e (Atlanta, Ga.: Fortnightly Insiders port), p. 4.

apoleon Hill and E. Harold Keown, *Suc-*͏d and Grow Rich Through Persuasion ͏ew York, N.Y., Fawcett World Library), p. ͏.

͏illiam Longgood, *Talking Your Way to Suc-*͏s — The Story of the Dale Carnegie Course ͏ew York, N.Y.: Association Press), p. 83.

⁴Claude Bristol, *The Magic of Believing* (Englewood Cliffs, N.J.: Prentice-Hall), p. 153.

⁵Elmer Wheeler, *How to Tap Your Hidden Sources of Energy* (New York, N.Y.: Castle Books), p. 60.

⁶David Schwartz, *The Magic of Thinking Big* (Englewood Cliffs, N.J.: Prentice-Hall), p. 140.

⁷Charles Conn, *The Possible Dream* (Old Tappan, N.J.: Fleming H. Revell Company), p. 171.

Performance coach **Anthony Robbins** teaches professionals how to *Sell with Certainty*. Robbins coached the turnaround of one of the United States' top financial traders. Robbins wrote *Unlimited Power*, *Awaken the Giant Within*, *Giant Steps* and *Notes from a Friend*. He produced the bestselling audio series of all time, *Personal Power*, with 24 million sold in less than five years as a result of his four TV infomercials. Peter Lynch and John Templeton have been instructors during his seminars. He spoke at Parliament before the House of Commons and the House of Lords. His philosophy for financial professionals is one of never-ending improvement. Robbins considers himself a "turnaround coach." He is one of the leading speakers to the financial industry.

Robbins One of Best Known, and Most Criticized, Motivational Speakers

Anthony Robbins has his cri͏ ics. Like Stephen Covey, he produce͏ a mountain of material for the peopl͏ who believe in his methods. He als͏ charges $12,000.00 per person for ͏ week-long session at his private i͏ land. Anthony Robbins' sessions usu͏ ally include a lot of cheerleading an͏ pep talks as well as opportunities t͏ meet like-minded people. However͏ some, like journalist Don Greenbur͏ of *Success Magazine*, have que͏ tioned the value of all this positivit͏

In 1991, Robbins was sued by h͏ franchise owners in Texas, Californi͏ and Georgia. The franchise owner͏ claimed that they were receiving a͏ unfairly small return and th͏ Robbins was getting the lion's shar͏ The FTC forced a settlement in fav͏ of the franchise owners.

In another suit, Wade B. Coo͏ author of *Wall Street Money Machin͏* alleged that Robbins plagiarized po͏ tions of his book. Cook won his su͏

While Anthony Robbins enjo͏ tremendous success, many consid͏ his info-mercials some of the mo͏ obnoxious of all time.

Author, consultant, speaker **Brian Tracy** has risen to the top of the crowded field of speakers and motivators who are available to corporations and professionals where sales are essential.

May you use what you have learned, to turn your life into a MASTERPIECE! If you do NOW what you KNOW you are suppose to and spell NOW backwards than you have WON! GOD LOVES YOU! Dr. Jan

www.ingramcontent.com/pod-product-compliance
Lightning Source LLC
Chambersburg PA
CBHW021955170526
45157CB00003B/1001